# SOVIET T-54
## MAIN BATTLE TANK

# SOVIET T-54
## MAIN BATTLE TANK

James Kinnear and Stephen L. (Cookie) Sewell

OSPREY PUBLISHING
Bloomsbury Publishing Plc
PO Box 883, Oxford, OX1 9PL, UK
1385 Broadway, 5th Floor, New York, NY 10018, USA
E-mail: info@ospreypublishing.com
**www.ospreypublishing.com**

OSPREY is a trademark of Osprey Publishing Ltd

First published in Great Britain in 2018

A catalogue record for this book is available from the British Library.

ISBN:     HB 978 1 4728 3330 3
          eBook 978 1 4728 3331 0
          ePDF 978 1 4728 3332 7
          XML 978 1 4728 3333 4

18 19 20 21 22    10 9 8 7 6 5 4 3 2 1

Index by Zoe Ross
Originated by PDQ Digital Media Solutions, Bungay, UK
Printed and bound in China by C&C Offset Printing., Ltd.

Front cover: (Upper) Soviet T-54B tanks on the march during winter exercises. (Lower) A column of Soviet T-54B tanks during summer exercises in the Soviet southern republics. Both author's collection.

Osprey Publishing supports the Woodland Trust, the UK's leading woodland conservation charity. Between 2014 and 2018 our donations are being spent on their Centenary Woods project in the UK.

To find out more about our authors and books visit **www.ospreypublishing.com**. Here you will find extracts, author interviews, details of forthcoming events and the option to sign up for our newsletter.

PICTURE CREDITS
All pictures are from the authors' collections unless otherwise noted. Artworks are by Andrey Aksenov and are credited where they appear.

ACKNOWLEDGEMENTS
The authors would like to acknowledge the assistance of many people, primarily located within the Russian Federation and Ukraine, for providing original Soviet and Russian source material and photographs for this book. In particular, thanks must go to Andrey Aksenov, Aleksandr Koshavtsev, Yuri Pasholok, Igor Zheltov and Sergei Popsuevich, all of whom provided what material they had available to ensure completeness of this work. With thanks also to Christopher Foss and Steven J. Zaloga for their assistance with material and advice on approaching the subject.

NOTE ON THE TRANSLATION AND PRONUNCIATION OF RUSSIAN LANGUAGE
The Russian alphabet has more characters than the Latin-based English language, and the Russian language is also grammatically complex, and subject to varying translation depending on context, gender, time period and nationality of the translator. Therefore, it is not always possible to directly translate Russian terms or names into English, and the various means of doing so are contentious and often arbitrary. Translations of some Russian terms have also been simplified in this book without the contentious pronunciation accents, as although perceived correct by those with an academic but no practical experience of the language, use outside a dry academic environment makes the subsequent English translation of a living Russian language difficult to read. An example is Ob'iekt (object) that has been simplified as Obiekt for consistency with previously published books. As these books are technical histories rather than studies of Russian grammar, the authors trust that this simplification of translation and terminology makes the books easier to read than would be the case if all the contentious accents were included.

# CONTENTS

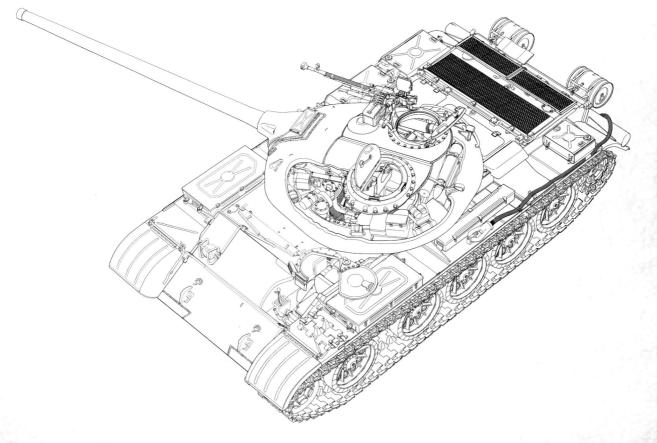

# INTRODUCTION

One of the most iconic and enduring symbols of Soviet military power during the early years of the Cold War was the silhouette of the T-54 tank on the streets of foreign capital cities during Soviet interventions in Europe, or crossing open terrain during massive Soviet armoured exercises. The sleek and unmistakable shape of the T-54 tank was a symbolic warning to any nation that wanted to stand against the Soviet empire.

But while the T-54 was a technological marvel of its day and a breakthrough in armoured vehicle design, the tank was essentially the perfect tank to fight World War II, or the 'Great Patriotic War' as it was known in the Soviet Union, and was not as technologically advanced as its initial appearance would suggest. In essence, the T-54 continued the Soviet wartime principle of designing relatively simple tanks that could be operated by crews with limited training. The post-war Soviet Army remained a conscript army, and as such the T-54 fitted the requirements of the Soviet Army perfectly.

During the service life of the tank, the T-54's monolithic homogenous armour became vulnerable to both the high explosive anti-tank warheads then being introduced on newly developed anti-tank guided missiles, and also the other major development used by NATO armies, armour-piercing discarding sabot (APDS) projectiles using dense core materials. When Soviet-built T-54 tanks began to clash with Western armour in proxy wars in South-East Asia and the Middle East, they were found to be on the losing end of many of the battles. This was in large part down to issues related to the training and deployment of the crews, and the ammunition types the Soviet Union chose to export, rather than an inherent problem with the T-54 tank design, which was a masterpiece of its time.

The T-54 tank was developed as a result of the collaborative efforts of several brilliant Soviet designers, as was typically the case with Soviet armoured vehicle designs. The lightweight and powerful 100mm D-10T gun was developed under the supervision of the famous designer F. F. Petrov, with the V-2 derived engine arrangement used in the T-54 was developed by a team headed by I. Ya. Trashutin. The overall T-54 concept was, however, in principle the brainchild of one man: Aleksandr Aleksandrovich Morozov. One of the three principal designers of the legendary T-34 tank, Morozov was personally motivated by the fact that the wartime tank was for historical purposes the brainchild of Mikhail Koshkin, and Morozov wanted to put his own stamp on the post-war Soviet tank industry with his own unique creation. Morozov would achieve this with the default Soviet Main Battle Tank (MBT) of the early Cold War – the T-54 – and would later go on to 'push the envelope' further, with the creation of the even more revolutionary T-64 series MBT.

The T-54 series was produced in large numbers in the Soviet Union, with the T-54 also being assembled in Poland, Czechoslovakia, and the People's Republic of China. The T-54 would also be the basis for the later T-55 re-design undertaken at Nizhny Tagil, and for later modernizations of the original Soviet T-54 design undertaken in China. This book will, however, address only the Soviet-built tanks and their derivatives such as the ZSU-57, SU-122-54, BTS armoured recovery vehicles and MTU bridge-layers.

Much of the credit for this book must be given to the research work undertaken by the Russian armour historians whose works have reached the West, analyzing much of the material from Soviet and Russian state archives that is not accessible to Western researchers. They include private Russian citizens as well as the official historians from both the Kharkov and Nizhny Tagil tank plants. Most of them will be identifiable from the bibliography used in the research for this book, but particular thanks must go to Andrey Aksenov, Yuri Pasholok and Colonel (retired) Igor Zheltov. Credit must also be given to acknowledged non-Russian experts in the field such as Steve Zaloga and Christopher Foss, who provided both information and advice on approaching this subject. The artwork was undertaken by Andrey Aksenov.

# CHAPTER ONE

## FIRST THERE WAS MOROZOV...

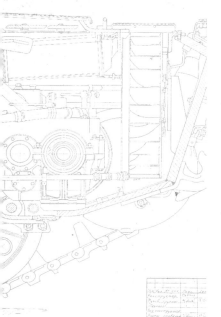

Many of the engineering geniuses of the Soviet era rose from humble beginnings. One of the greatest of them was Aleksandr Aleksandrovich Morozov (1904–79). Born near Bryansk, he completed his elementary schooling and at the age of 14 went to the Kharkov Railway Locomotive Construction Plant (KhPZ – also known as the Kharkov 'Komintern' Locomotive Plant) to learn the trade of building steam locomotives. He began work at the plant just as the Russian Revolution was taking effect across what would become the Soviet Union, but despite many of his colleagues joining the Bolshevik Party, Morozov did not join the VKP (b) Communist (Bolshevik) party until 1943, which clearly did no harm to his post-war career.

After beginning as an apprentice draftsman, Morozov was assigned to the nascent tank design bureau at KhPZ to work on the T-12 medium tank project. He was sent by his supervisor, M. V. Lomonosov, to the Kharkov Machinery Construction Technical Academy for advanced training from 1929 to 1931. On his return to the plant, he began work on the transmissions and drivelines for the new BT fast tank series, and by 1936 was the chief designer for tank running gear at the plant. When the great purges affected the plant in 1937, the chief designer at KhPZ was one of the victims, but Morozov was not, as he expected, promoted to chief designer, the position being given instead to a new designer, a graduate of the Leningrad Polytechnic Institute by the name of Mikhail Koshkin. The two men thereafter co-operated well together, but Morozov inevitably resented that he had not been made chief engineer, and this resentment carried over to later projects in which Morozov was involved.

Koshkin was by 1937 already a particularly experienced designer, and had been awarded the Order of the Red Star for his design work in Leningrad. On his arrival in Kharkov in 1937 he set about the task of designing an improved version of the BT-20 wheel-and-track tank that KhPZ had been assigned to develop. The 'improvement' emerged as the A-32 medium tank design, which, after testing and further modification as the A-34, was approved for production as the T-34 medium tank. The new tank combined all of the best ideas of the day – a powerful 76.2mm tank gun, steeply sloped armour, wide tracks, Christie suspension inherited from the BT fast tank series and the BD-2 (later V-2) high speed diesel engine. Morozov was responsible for the transmission on the new tank, which was troublesome on early production tanks, but was rectified as experience with the new design grew.

Koshkin had been under severe strain while developing the new T-34 tank, and he fell seriously ill with pneumonia while accompanying the original T-34 prototypes on their trial run to Moscow for presentation to the Soviet hierarchy, including Stalin. The combined effects of work-related stress and pneumonia took their toll, and Koshkin died in September 1940. Morozov was thereafter named as the new chief designer for the T-34 tank, and would retain that position until the tank left production in 1946.

Problems with initial series production of the T-34 led to the consideration of alternative designs. As war loomed on the horizon, a decision was taken in Moscow (on behalf of Kotin, the chief designer of LKZ, the Leningrad Kirov Plant) to consider replacement of the Kharkov T-34 design with a significantly modified design, the T-34M, which resembled an enlarged version of the T-50 light tank produced in Leningrad. The T-34M was not, however, developed to production stage due to the German invasion in June 1941.

In October 1941, as Axis forces closed on Kharkov, the KhPZ plant (now known as Plant No. 183) was evacuated to Nizhny Tagil, together with the Morozov design team, the plant production engineers and their families. The plant was merged with the Ural Railway Wagon Construction Plant (UVZ, colloquially known as 'Vagonka' to its workers) in October 1941 in order to continue production there of the T-34 medium tank. Morozov oversaw production of the tank, but, aware of the field maintenance difficulties being encountered by operational units due to the different parts being produced at six separate plants, he demanded to be given direct control of all design changes as many parts of the seemingly identical T-34 tanks were not interchangeable. His request was granted and Morozov became the ruling authority over UVZ and overall T-34 standardization and production.

The original T-34 was well designed, with a wide fighting compartment deck and a powerful V-2 diesel engine, and as such was easily modified later in the war to mount a larger calibre 85mm gun in an enlarged and heavier

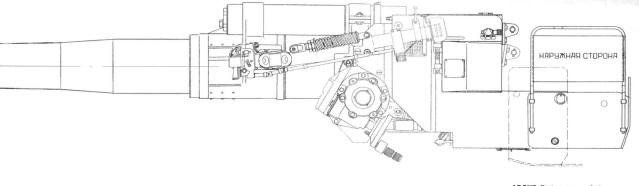

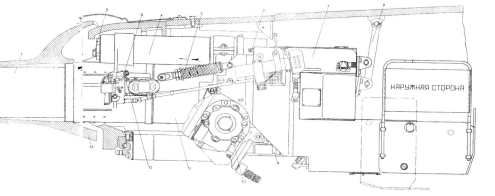

НАРУЖНАЯ СТОРОНА

**ABOVE** Side view of the D-10T gun. This was a unitary weapon and as such required lifting the turret and removal of the gun to change out the barrel and breech assembly when required.

**LEFT** Close-up from the manual of the D-10T and TSh2-22 sight, showing how the sight was hinged, with prisms for use by the gunner.

turret with a larger diameter turret race. The new turret, developed under Morozov's supervision, allowed for the accommodation of a very welcome third member of the turret crew.

Morozov was, however, cognizant that he had improved an inherited tank design, and wanted to come up with a new design that he could call his own and that was superior to all other current tank designs. He well understood the engineering problems that needed to be overcome to produce an entirely new tank.

One of the main concerns was the overall combat weight of the new tank design. If the tank was to be fitted with heavy armour to protect it against 88mm projectiles – at the time the greatest threat – it would inevitably become heavier and therefore need a longer track run on the ground to maintain adequate ground pressure. But that introduced a counteracting problem in that the longer the track run the less manoeuvrable the tank was in combat. Both the Soviet T-35 and the French Char 2C had proven nearly impossible to turn in an acceptable manner due to that very problem.

Morozov's solution was for the day somewhat radical: the engine – a 12-cylinder V-2 diesel – would be mounted transversely in the engine bay and a transfer case used to transmit power to the transmission, thus shortening the overall hull length. As a result the tank would be shorter and thereby lighter, while still able to have increased glacis armour and mount a heavier turret also providing better armour protection.

Morozov began consideration of such a T-34 replacement in late 1942, but due to wartime production priorities was not able to develop the concept until much later. The T-43 was developed to prototype stage, but did not offer sufficient advantages over the T-34 in a mass production priority wartime environment, so was ultimately abandoned. The T-43 incorporated many of Morozov's new ideas, however, and in particular adopted the much more compact torsion bar suspension. Further development work resulted in a new hull design and transverse engine arrangement, which also developed under Morozov's direct supervision. This tank ultimately emerged as the T-44 medium tank, which entered into production at the recaptured and re-commissioned Kharkov plant in November 1944. The tank had a significant number of what in Russian is termed *detskye bolezni* or 'children's diseases' (teething troubles) and was assembled at a low production rate, by Soviet standards. No T-44 tanks are known to have seen service in World War II, with 1,800 being built in total in the immediate post-war months.

In the meantime, the Soviet military in the final months of the war considered the 85mm tank gun as a weapon that, while suitable as an interim armament, would nevertheless not be as effective against emerging threats. The preferred option was the new 100mm D-10T tank gun designed by F. F. Petrov, utilizing a naval calibre used on Soviet destroyers, and via considerable argument and intrigue ultimately based on the D-10S originally mounted in the SU-100 self-propelled gun.

After testing of what was designated the T-44-100, the decision was taken to re-design the tank to accept the new armament in a new turret, while simultaneously remedying some of the flaws of the T-44 series. On 1 November 1944, the People's Commissar for Tank Production of the Soviet Union, Vyacheslav A. Malyshev, signed off on Order No. 0637 for the creation of a new tank, the T-54, with Morozov and his team based at Nizhny Tagil ordered to build a prototype of the new tank.

The first prototype of the new T-54 tank was completed by the Nizhny Tagil plant on 30 January 1945. The tank was heavily based on the T-44 and used the same T-34 type driveline with two-link track elements and a roller engagement drive sprocket along with a particularly contoured new cast turret to mount the 100mm armament. This tank, later known as the T-54 Model 1945, was sent to Kubinka between 11 March and 14 April 1945 for testing under the watchful eye of the legendary Colonel Ye. A. Kulchitsky. On 8 December 1945, the test findings were published and the Nizhny Tagil plant ordered to build two more prototypes for additional testing along with the design drawings for series production by no later than 1 June 1946.

The new task team formed to work on the T-54 project included the engineers Ya. I. Baran, N. M. Chistyakov, V. D. Volkov, G. S. Mironov, I. A. and M. A. Nabutovsky, Yu. A. Kholudin, V. D. Gaplevsky, M. G. Kizin, and T. I. Libun. At the time the team was being formed, many of the designers previously evacuated to Nizhny Tagil including Morozov himself were petitioning to return to their former homes in Kharkov, which had an inevitable impact on the development of the T-54.

The revised T-54 design maintained many of the features of the T-54 Model 1945, but changed the T-34 style tracks for a toothed drive sprocket system, using narrower cast tracks. On 29 April 1946, the T-54 tank was accepted for service with the Soviet Army in accordance with Resolution No. 960-402 of the Council of Ministers of the USSR (SM SSSR) and the Politburo. There remained a large number of problems with the tank design, however, and production output was particularly slow while the tank was undergoing continuous testing and modification at Nizhny Tagil based on trials at the Kubinka Test Range. In the meantime, the Commissariat for Tank Production (NKTP) had been dissolved and in its place the Ministry of Transport Machinery Construction (MTrM) had been formed on 9 May 1946. The new ministry was still under the leadership of V. A. Malyshev, but others had been elevated to the membership of its leadership council, including the former UVZ plant manager Yu. Ye. Maksarev. The engineer Nikolai A. Kucherenko, who had worked with Koshkin and Morozov on the T-34 design, would become chief designer of MTrM between 1947 and 1949 before moving to the UVZ plant as chief designer from 1949 to 1952. He was given two Stalin awards (1st rank in 1946 and 2nd rank in 1948) for his involvement in the T-54 design.

After a meeting on the T-54 project held in Moscow on 17 June 1946, Morozov noted that by mutual agreement of all involved parties the T-54 would require considerable re-design before entering series production. This was duly undertaken, and by 11 October 1946, Morozov noted that his engineers had reduced the weight of the tank to 34.97 metric tonnes, nearly four metric tonnes lighter than the original T-54 prototype.

The first T-54 Model 1947 prototype underwent testing, with the test reports published on 30 March 1947. While many of the initial design

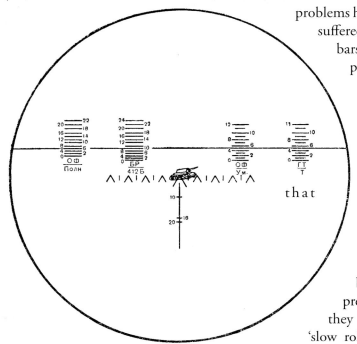

that

The reticule from the TSh2-22 sight, showing the various range compensation scales for HE (full charge), AP, HE (reduced charge) and machine gun. The carat symbols are for use when tracking a moving target.

problems had been corrected, the new prototype suffered from stress fracturing of the torsion bars and road wheel arms. While these problems were corrected and the tank approved for full series production by MTrM Order No. 00252 dated 15 October 1947, some problems remained unresolved.

One of the main technical issues with the T-54 M-1947 was TsNII-48 – the State Armour Development and Testing Institute – disliked the original turret design, as although it provided an excellent overall ballistic shape, the lower surfaces presented some shot traps. As a result they did what today is sometimes called 'slow rolling' the production until a better turret design could be devised.

At the same time Morozov had proposed a 'T-64' tank design, based on the same T-54 chassis and turret but fitted with the proposed V-64 flat-opposed-piston diesel engine. Though not developed at the time, the idea was carried over to the new and revolutionary T-64 tank design later in the 1950s.

The alternative TsNII-48 turret proposals emerged in March 1949 as the T-54 Model 1949, with a new narrow pig snout aperture and gun mantlet for the 100mm armament and a turret front without any shot traps; however, the turret rear featured an undercut to reduce weight, which retained such a shot-trap potential. This was finally corrected in 1951 with the definitive turret shape and production model of the T-54 series, the T-54 Model 1951.

While these design changes were taking place, Morozov was pleading with Moscow to let him return to Kharkov and reform their design bureau. Morozov was also at the time not in good health. After agreeing to spend two weeks in a Moscow sanatorium, Morozov was permitted to return to Kharkov and form the design bureau for Plant No. 75.

T-54 tanks produced at Kharkov, in contrast with the high level of quality control achieved at Nizhny Tagil, suffered from quality-related production problems, which led to early-production tanks suffering issues with military acceptance. Morozov ascribed the problems to the poor quality of the personnel and 'production traits' of the workers. He argued that both he and the military gave the actual tanks high marks and it was only these problems, and not endemic issues with the tank itself, that needed correction.

As with the T-34 before it, the T-54 received a constant stream of complaints and recommendations for improvement as feedback from operational Soviet Army service, which were acted upon to improve the design. One of many minor problems was with dimensional errors made in the machining of the 'guitara', the transfer case for the engine/transmission – the component so named due to being shaped like the body of a guitar. Not surprisingly, the primary mission assigned to Plant No. 75 by the MTrM in 1952 was improving the quality control of T-54 tank production at that plant.

As the T-54 was entering series production in its definitive form, Morozov was meantime pressing on with an even more radical tank design, Obiekt 430, which would eventually become the T-64 Main Battle Tank. According to Morozov's own memoirs, after 1953 he left further development and modification of the T-54 to his subordinates while he concentrated on the Article 430 and the later Article 432 designs.

In 1952 Morozov had also argued with MTrM in Moscow to relocate his favourite deputy, Yakov 'Yari' Baran, from Nizhny Tagil to Kharkov. MTrM wanted Baran to replace Kucherenko at Nizhny Tagil, but Morozov was insistent and finally won his case. Baran moved to Kharkov and as a result the new designer at Nizhny Tagil became Leonid I. Kartsev, who would prove to be the antithesis of Morozov, with a completely different philosophy on tank design. While Morozov worked on the T-64 MBT in Kharkov, Kartsev's alternative T-72 tank design would become one of the most prolific post-war tanks built in the Soviet Union after the T-54 and T-55 series. Over the years, the clash in design philosophies would be seen as 'revolutionary' or high-risk designs from Morozov in Kharkov versus 'evolutionary' or safe designs developed by Kartsev in Nizhny Tagil. Kartsev's own first tank design was the T-55 Model 1958, which he referred to as a 'rationalization' of all of the ideas used in the T-54, with a number of necessary corrections and upgrades required to make it a better tank overall. But that is an entire subject in its own right. Morozov continued in his capacity of chief designer in the city until he retired in 1976. He died in retirement in Kharkov on 14 June 1979.

# CHAPTER TWO
## DEVELOPMENT OF THE T-54 MEDIUM TANK

After the initial devastation of Operation *Barbarossa*, and once production of the T-34 tank had been re-established on the production lines in Nizhny Tagil, Stalingrad and the 'Krasnoye Sormovo' plant in Gorky, Morozov began to consider a successor tank that would improve on its combat qualities and be better suited to combat new German tank developments. While the Pz.Kpfw. VI 'Tiger 1' only began to appear on the Eastern Front in November 1942 and the 'Elefant' and 'Panther' would not arrive until the battle of Kursk in the summer of 1943, overall improvements as always in tank development showed a need for a better tank for the future. Even now the Pz.Kpfw. III had been upgraded, initially to a short-barrelled L/42 and then a long-barrelled L/60 5cm gun, and the Pz.Kpfw. IV had gone from a short-barrelled L/24 gun to first an L/43 and then an L/48 gun. Both of these new weapons gave them a much better chance to defeat the T-34 at longer engagement ranges.

As related in the previous chapter, Morozov's initial attempt to improve the T-34 was the T-43 tank project. The tank was an improved version of the T-34 tank, modified with torsion bar suspension that permitted the hull to be lower while also providing an additional 30cm of lateral internal space. In its second iteration the T-43 was also provided with a three-man turret, which would permit the tank commander to function in his primary role as commander without having also to perform as gunner. Other modifications included changing the driver-mechanic's position over to the right side of the hull and elimination of the hull

Prototype No. 2 of the first version of the T-54, with the early T-34 style running gear. Note the T-34/44 style headlight on the left side of the hull.

Side view of the T-54 Model 1945 prototype, showing the T-34 type running gear.

machine gun. While the T-43 tank was generally considered a successful design, the State declined to produce the tank as it was too close to the original T-34 in overall performance characteristics to warrant a changeover in production tooling, with the inevitable loss of existing production output as the changes were made. The T-43 project was therefore cancelled.

The developments undertaken on the T-43 would not be wasted, however. Morozov's 'universal turret' with a three-man turret crew configuration was also used for a modified and larger turret that was developed in parallel. The turret as used in the T-34-85 was a three-man turret in which the gunner and commander were seated in tandem on the left side with the loader on the right. The earlier 'universal turret', which was capable of mounting either the 76.2mm F-34 gun or the new 85mm D-5T tank gun, was used as the basis for the T-34-85 turret that emerged in late 1943 armed with the D-5T gun. A further modified T-34-85 turret went into series production in January 1944 armed with the ZiS-S-53 gun.

In the autumn of 1943 Morozov and KB-520 (the UVZ design bureau) went to work on Morozov's proposed 'revolutionary' medium tank. KB-520 was tasked to provide a highly manoeuvrable tank with excellent armour protection, with a combat weight of around 30 metric tonnes, a turret race diameter of 1,800mm, and to present a much lower silhouette compared with the T-34. Approved by NKTP Order No. 705ss dated 22 November 1943, the new tank was designated the T-44, and two prototypes were to be built by 1 February 1944.

In order to provide for all of the requirements and keep it shorter overall, the new tank used a transverse layout for its V-2-44 engine and a transfer case (the aforementioned 'guitara') to drive the transmission at the rear of the hull. The MTO engine-transmission compartment layout was relatively compact, with the exhaust now exiting from a large port on the left side, and with the transfer case and crankshaft output on the right side. Initially the hull had a combination hatch and viewer for the driver-mechanic on the left front side of the hull, but as the tank evolved it was replaced with a round lid-type hatch and two simple viewers for him facing forward with a view block to the left side. The drive sprockets and tracks from the T-34 series were initially used on the new design. A modified turret, similar to that used on the T-34-85, was fitted to the new hull.

The tank went through considerable testing and modification as the original design evolved. Changes included mounting the ZiS-S-53 85mm gun as a standard armament option, and a version designated T-44-122, which mounted the 122mm D-25T tank gun. While there was some talk of using 90mm glacis armour instead of 75mm, the 75mm glacis was ultimately adopted. Testing was concluded on 18 July 1944, with production planned at both the newly re-commissioned Plant No. 75 (formerly the Kharkov Diesel Engine Plant) and Plant No. 264 NKTP in Stalingrad. Production output was planned to reach 300 tanks per month by May 1945; however, this was never realised due to the end of the war in Europe on 25 April 1944. While all of this was going on, A. I. Blagonravov wrote his conclusions on the new T-44 and proposed that it should be followed at once by a new tank – the T-54 – with a number of changes to the design, including a turret similar in shape to the new IS-3 heavy tank prototypes, a synchronized transmission with two-speed transfer case, protection from 'Panzerfaust'-type shaped charge weapons, a steeper rear hull plate, a rotating turret floor, and a commander's cupola with multiple vision devices similar to the late production Sherman M4A2 tanks now arriving via Lend-Lease. He also recommended re-consideration of locating a ZPU or anti-aircraft machine-gun mounting on the turret. While it took time, as will be seen nearly all of these items would eventually appear in the design of the T-54 tank. The project to work on a new T-54 MBT was approved by NKTP on 10 October 1944.

The specifications for the new T-54 tank were put forth on 1 November 1944 by NKTP Order No. 637s. The order related the basic points required to upgrade from the T-44 design, including installation of the powerful 100mm D-10T tank gun, using 120mm thick upper and lower glacis armour with the lower glacis being reset to 50–55° versus 45° on the

A T-54 model 1947 tank after modernization in 1960s. Remotely controlled SG-43 machine guns were removed from the mudguards, and a standard set of tool/spare-part boxes and external fuel tanks installed. From an unknown tank unit of the Soviet Army during the 1960s. (Andrey Aksenov)

T-44, a turret with 150mm armour protection, electric power for turret and gun training, a 12.7mm DShK heavy machine gun mount on the turret, wider wheels with rubber rims, and increased working room for the crew within the tank. As a bonus to give the designers a stimulus, Morozov was apparently given 30 gents' suits to hand out to the designers as a gift.

Plant No. 183 (UVZ) also proposed two new models of the T-44, the T-44A, which was a third prototype armed with an 85mm gun tank, and the T-44-100, which was to mount the 100mm D-10T gun derived from the D-10S that had been developed for the SU-100. The T-44A was judged superior to the original version and was adopted for production instead, but was simply designated the T-44 tank when it entered production. This was the tank accepted for service with the Red Army by GKO Resolution No. 6997 dated 23 November 1944 and which entered production in Kharkov, with five tanks being completed that month. By the end of 1945, 265 T-44s had been built; however, production was terminated in 1947, at which time only 1,800 T-44s had been produced in total.

The T-44 had a somewhat chequered career in the Soviet Army, but did make at least one 'combat' appearance during the 1956 Warsaw Pact suppression of the uprising in Hungary. Other than that, T-44 tanks spent most of their time being used for training purposes. A mid-life upgrade,

designated the T-44M, partially standardized the T-44 with the then-current T-54 tanks by fitting them with new external fuel tanks and a narrower version of the cast OMSh tracks with toothed drive sprockets as well as new electrical components. T-44 tanks were later rebuilt as BTS-4 high-speed tank-recovery tractors.

The fate of the T-44-100 was quite different. This tank was initially developed by Morozov in the summer of 1945 and was envisaged as a further development of the T-44. After experimenting with the gun on a standard T-44 chassis, it was found to need a number of changes, and the result is in some sources referred to as the T-44B.

The new tank design (now formally designated as the T-54) had significant promise and was recommended by the test commission for acceptance for service with the Red Army as the T-54 medium tank after a number of test findings were corrected per Soviet standard practice.

On 11 April 1945 the results of the testing of the new T-54 prototype, again conducted under the control of Colonel Ye. A. Kulchitsky, were released. According to the plant history of the tank, his main findings were:

1.   The T-54 tank, which is presented as a modernized T-44 tank, in its own primary combat qualities (the power of its armament and armour protection) is superior to all other corresponding medium tanks.

2. Range testing to a total of 1,553km has verified the durability of the primary mechanical components of the prototype model T-54 tank. But at the same time testing has established the necessity of developing (improving) a number of components and assemblies.

3. The primary shortcoming of the T-54 tank relates to the insufficient penetration resistance of the turret and the obsolete design of the transmission and running gear, which is unacceptable for a modern tank. The turret can be damaged at long ranges, and the transmission and running gear reduce the dynamic qualities of the tank.

4. By studying the sharply increased combat qualities of the medium tank, as achieved by the T-54 tank, the commission considers it worthwhile to recommend the T-54 tank for acceptance into service with the Soviet Army with the obligation to correct the above-mentioned shortcomings.

5. In connection with this, and so that a host of new components may be introduced into the series production of the T-54, the commission considers the possibility of commencing production of the T-54 tanks without waiting for the introduction of the following components and mechanisms, the immediate development of which is ordered for Plant No. 183 to carry out in the order determined by the NKTP and GBTU KA:

a) A turret similar to that used by the IS-3;

b) A gearbox with synchronizer and a 2-speed planetary steering mechanism

c) A screen to protect from 'Faustpatrone' (Panzerfaust);

d) Changes to the angle of slope of the rear hull plates;

e) A rotating floor in the fighting compartment;

f) (Sherman) M4A2 type vision devices in the commander's cupola;

g) Tracks using a toothed wheel drive;

h) Shock absorbers for the running gear (on all road wheels).

As he noted, one of the main complaints involved getting rid of the T-34 type track drive and replacing it with a new design using toothed drive sprockets and tracks with openings for engagement of those drive sprockets. This emerged with the use of the 12-spine 'spider' wheels that were similar to those of the T-44 but dimensionally different, with new drive sprockets and the narrow version of what eventually became the OMSh open metal hinge cast tracks. This second prototype version appeared in July 1945 (in 1952 it was then designated Obiekt 137; the T-34 became Obiekt 135 and the T-44 Obiekt 136 in retroactive designations).

Among other things contemplated for the new tank undergoing development was a gun stabilizer system. Lend-Lease Sherman tanks provided to the Soviet union had a rudimentary system installed and it proved to be useful, so the Soviet Army wanted to work on its own design. This was first proposed on 17 October 1946 in Resolution No. 2287-957 SM SSSR for the T-44 armed with the 85mm gun, but, given the fact that this development was a dead end due to the termination of T-44 production, it was changed over to the new T-54 tank in 1947. The STP-34 and STP-S-53 gun stabilizing systems were developed during 1943–45 for T-34s, with many more experiments undertaken in the background. Also proposed for the new tank (after testing on the proposed T-34-100 tank project) was a new fire control system using a Russian version of the 'Cadillac' fire controls that were being installed in American tanks. This was designated as the PUOR-4 but was not perfected until many years later.

First and foremost the T-54 needed to become a viable tank. One of the principal design decisions was whether to use the 100mm LB-1 or the 100mm D-10T gun as main armament. While the LB-1 was preferred, the barrel was approximately 1 metre longer, and during trials the muzzle brake produced clouds of dust, which revealed the tank's position, so further work was required. There were fewer problems foreseen with the proven D-10T, which was already in service (as the 100mm D-10S) on the SU-100 self-propelled gun, and the D-10T was duly chosen for the new T-54 tank.

The first three prototypes (T-54 'Model 1946' tanks in some sources) were used to prove the original concept and design and to determine faults that would arise during testing. The first prototype from January 1945 was reworked, with the second prototype incorporating many of the recommendations made during initial testing. Testing of the second prototype lasted from 28 July 1945 to 4 November 1945. Fuel capacity was increased to 545 litres and external fuel capacity increased from 165 to 180 litres (total 725 litres), but, due to an increase in combat weight from 35.5 to 39.15 metric tonnes, range was still only 300–360km. No main armament was installed during the trials, as there was still an ongoing debate over which gun design to use.

An establishment lot (*ustanovochnaya partiya*) was ordered for assembly by 15 March 1946. Even without intensive service testing, the SM SSSR passed Resolution No. 960-402ss on 29 April 1946 that accepted the T-54 medium tank for production and service with the Soviet Army (the Red Army was re-designated as the Soviet Army in February 1946). Production was slated to begin in September 1946 and 165 tanks were to be produced by 31 December of that year. However, only two more prototypes (numbers

**ABOVE** The sixth T-54 prototype that with its test 'findings' corrected became the production model T-54 Model 1947.

**RIGHT** A series production model T-54 Model 1947 in standard service configuration.

3 and 4) were ready in July 1946 and they underwent testing from 20 July 1946 to 10 August 1946 at Nizhny Tagil. Each tank had a different gun installation (100mm LB-1 and 100mm D-10T) and after this they were sent for comparative artillery testing. The D-10T finally won and was designated as the main armament for the new tank by SM SSSR Resolution No. 2198-897s on 30 September 1946.

It was only with the fourth prototype that the new T-54 tank began to take shape. The first two lead production tanks (Nos. 5 and 6) underwent plant testing at UVZ from 24 April to 27 May 1947. The tanks, serial numbers 470106 and 470208, still had some design problems that were noted in the plant assessment by Morozov and Kucherenko. But in July the plant began to gear up for series production. After the tank finally entered production late that year, the tank was ultimately built in three series (T-54 Models 1947, 1949 and 1951) with a grand total of 10,245 line tanks built between 1947 and 1955. But with all of its teething troubles the T-54 was only finally given full acceptance for service with the Soviet Army on 12 June 1950 by Defence Ministry Order No. 112.

The first production tank series, the T-54 Model 1947, was produced from July 1947 to January 1949 when production was terminated per Council of Ministers Resolution No. 313-109 dated 26 January 1949. A total of 617 early models were built for Soviet Army service, with 96 more assembled specifically for use as training tanks. The basic componentry of the tank was present from this early model – driver-mechanic and ammunition storage in the bow, fighting compartment with a three-man crew in the centre, and the compact engine-transmission compartment (MTO) in the rear. Unlike later tanks, the tank retained the 'wing' machine guns used on the prototypes, with a remote control 7.62mm SG-43 machine gun mounted behind the mud guards on each front track guard. The tank also had a third 7.62mm SG-43 mounted in the turret as a coaxial weapon, and a 12.7mm DShKM machine gun on a Tourelle mount[*] that was swung over the loader's hatch when required. A construction nuance is that, starting in October 1947, the tank switched from the use of butt-joint welded glacis plates to the use of interlocking dovetailed plates, which would remain a signature of the tank throughout its production life.

An assessment by the Chief of Tank Troops of the Soviet Army, Marshal Bogdanov, showed that the new tank outgunned the US M26 tank of the day while still being 6–9 metric tonnes lighter, plus it had superior armour protection. Most of the early-production T-54 tanks were used to equip the 5th Guards Tank Army. Troops generally liked the tank, but there were a number of defects with it due to production and design failings, not least of which was poor off-road mobility compared with the earlier T-34-85. The number of defects on early series production tanks was so bad that production was temporarily halted in 1949. The defects that required attention included

[*]    From the French for turret, but also attributed to a ball-race ring mount allowing a secondary weapon, usually a machine gun, to be rotated through 360°.

disintegration of the gearbox internals, constantly breaking torsion bars, poor incoming air filtration for the engine, and problems with the fire suppression system that either released spontaneously or did not work at all when urgently needed. All series production tanks were also over their design weight, at best by 140kg, and sometimes by up to 1 metric tonne.

An analysis by the Central Research Institute for Armour (TsNII-48) showed the turret design of the new tank was dreadful from a protection standpoint. Due to its 'sculpted' lines the turret featured an all round shot trap, which the Russians knew from World War II experience could easily cause the turret to be jammed or sheared off the tank by impacting enemy projectiles. The institute proposed a new design, which underwent testing from late 1948 into 1949. After receiving approval for the first variation of this new design, which included other modifications to the tank determined during operational use of the first batch of tanks, the new tank, now designated T-54 Model 1949, was authorized for production in accordance with SM SSSR Resolution No. 2620-1039 dated 18 June 1949.

This tank entered production at Plant No. 183 (Nizhny Tagil) in October and at Plant No. 75 (Kharkov) and Plant No. 174 (Omsk) in November 1949. During its production run at all three plants a total of 2,523 T-54 Model 1949 tanks were manufactured.

The new version now had a lighter combat weight of 35.5–36 metric tonnes and used a new cast turret with a nearly hemispherical front shape with a much narrower aperture for the gun and 'pig snout' mantlet. The coaxial machine gun and telescopic sight now required their own separate ports for installation in the turret, but the overall level of protection was far higher than that of the T-54 Model 1947. The glacis armour was, however, reduced from 120mm to 100mm together with other changes that reduced the combat weight of the tank from 39.15 metric tonnes on the T-54 Model 1947 to around 37.5 metric tonnes on the T-54 M-1949. The twin 7.62mm SG-43 'wing' guns were changed for a single fixed 7.62mm SG-43 located to the right of the driver-mechanic's compartment. The anti-aircraft mount was also changed to a built-in rotating tourelle on the loader's hatch in place of the swing-over type ring used on the T-54 Model 1947. Internally many components were also upgraded, such as the installation of a PPO fire suppression system.

An assessment completed by the Chief of Tank Troops on 28 July 1949 indicated that the Soviet Army saw a need for a total of 19,196 T-54 tanks, but only 700 were actually in service at that time. Clearly, production would need to be ramped up exponentially to meet the demands. But even at that time testing conducted in August 1949 showed that the modified turret was very unbalanced, which required a great deal of effort for the gunner to traverse the turret when the tank was on a slope. It also retained a significant shot trap at the rear.

Late in their service lives, T-54 Model 1949 tanks underwent capital rebuilding and as a result were brought nearly up to the level of equipment fitted to the T-54A or T-54B tanks, depending on when they were upgraded. Particularly worn tanks that were not upgraded were converted to BTS-4A repair and recovery vehicles.

A second attempt at modernization was made in 1950 per SM SSSR Resolution No. 2468-983 dated 10 June 1950, which included a new turret design from TsNII-48. After testing conducted from 27 February to 7 March 1951, the new version, designated T-54 Model 1951, was approved for production. Series production of the modified design began in November 1951 at all three plants and continued until May 1955, with a total of 7,009 tanks of this type being built. Prices per tank were 415,000 roubles from Plant No. 75, 455,000 roubles from Plant No. 183, and 485,000 roubles from Plant No. 174. For comparison, a T-44 cost only 230,000 roubles from Plant No. 75.

As was identified by Blagonravov back in 1944 referring to an IS-3 type turret design, the new T-54 turret now resembled a nearly complete hemisphere with no shot traps anywhere, with subtle changes made to the

A T-54 Model 1947 from the left rear, with all fuel tanks, stowage bins and smoke canisters in place.

location of internal elements in an attempt to make the turret better balanced and thereby easier for the gunner to traverse. The turret was slightly asymmetric to the left to accommodate the gunner and commander, but the design permitted the gun to remain on the tank's centreline. During its production run a significant number of detail changes were made to the tank, including permitting adjustable louvres for the radiator air intake and exhaust grills and the use of improved vision devices.

The T-54K commander's tank entered production starting with the Model 1949, for use by regimental level and higher commanders. Under the designation Obiekt R-50 the first models were created in the summer of 1948, with the first production versions rolling off the Plant No. 183 production line in early September 1950. A follow-on version was authorized by SM SSSR Order No. 6286s dated 22 March 1952, and two models were built on the Model 1951 chassis in early 1954 by Plant No. 183. But it was not until 1958 that they were accepted for service, with 50 T-54K Model 1951 tanks being built at Omsk. These tanks were fitted with an RSB-3T radio system for use as command tanks as well as the standard 10RT-26Eh short-range tank-to-tank radio set. During capital rebuild in later years, the 10RT-26Eh was replaced by the new R-113 VHF set, the RSB-3T by an R-112 HF set, and the TPU by an R-120 intercom system. The tanks also received a GAB-1-P/30 generator set.

A T-54 Model 1947, T-54 Model 1951 and a BTR-60P on exercise. Most Soviet Army units did not differentiate between tank models, referring to all tanks simply as T-54.

The endeavour to fit Soviet tanks with gun stabilizer systems began to reach fruition in 1952–53 with prototype models of the STP-1 'Gorizont' vertical axis stabilizer undergoing testing. This was a joint effort between Plant No. 183 and the TsNII-173 Electronic Research Institute, with three prototype tanks assembled in May 1952, and testing taking place in August of that year before handover for government testing.

In 1954 the UVZ plant in Nizhny Tagil assembled 25 tanks as an establishment lot for the new concept. Per SM SSSR Resolution No. 420-260 dated 8 March 1955, the new tank (Obiekt 137G or now designated the T-54A tank) was accepted for service and production for the Soviet Army. The tank entered production at the three T-54 production plants, and between 1 June 1955 and the fourth quarter of 1957 (October–December) 4,602 of these tanks were built.

The modified T-54A tank was nearly identical externally to the late production T-54 Model 1951, but the new D-10TG gun had a new sight and a fume extractor added at the end of the gun in addition to the stabilizer within the turret. The tank was also now fitted with night driving equipment. Most of the other controls and components remained the same. But early in the production run the 12-fin 'spider' wheels used for the entire production run of the tank from 1947 onwards began to be replaced with a new five-spoke 'starfish' cast wheel. This is reflected on the original blueprints for the tank

dated 1956. However, due to large inventories of 'spider' wheels, tanks were built with both types for some time, according to available inventory.

As with the T-54 M-1951, there was likewise a command variant of the T-54A, the T-54AK tank, which was accepted for service in 1958, with 50 command tanks being built that year by Plant No. 183. The tank repeated the late T-54K layout with an R-113, R-112 and R-120 but used a new 'Ural-180' auxiliary generator.

During the same period that the T-54A was under development, a second stabilizer-equipped tank, the T-54B, was undergoing development. This tank was developed in response to SM SSSR resolutions No. 1552-545 dated 29 March 1952 and No. 347-205 dated 5 March 1955. This tank, given the industrial designator Obiekt 137G2, was fitted with a mock-up of the STP-2 'Tsiklon' two-axis stabilizer in the summer of 1954. The man responsible for the successful installation of the system was the engineer Yury Kostenko. The tank completed range and troop testing in February 1956 and was approved for production per SM SSSR Resolution No. 1118-581 dated 15 August 1956. Production took place from July 1957 to June 1958 at Plant No. 183, from 1 January 1958 to March 1959 at Plant No. 75, and only from July to September 1957 at Plant No. 174. In total, 1,555 T-54B tanks were built.

The T-54B was externally very similar to the T-54A but featured an infrared headlight for night driving using the driver's TVN-2 night vision device. Soon after the tank was approved for production, in 1959, it was also fitted with a TPN-1 night sight for the gunner and a TPK-1 night sight for the commander, as well as an L-2 infrared searchlight on a bracket welded to the gun mantlet. Later a smaller OU-3 searchlight for use by the commander would be added to his cupola. The upgraded T-54A, Model 1951 and Model 1949 tanks also received the same night sight as well as a modified searchlight mount on the turret to the right of the gun that was linked to the gun barrel to adjust its elevation.

Another change on this tank model was the moving of the BDSh-5 smoke canisters to the rear mud guards, allowing racks to be mounted on the rear plate for carrying two 200-litre fuel tanks to extend the tank's overall range. These canisters were not attached to the internal fuel system, with fuel being transferred to the external or internal fuel tanks to extend the tank's range via the use of a hand pump. The tank crew was theoretically supposed to remove these tanks before entering combat and replace them with the BDSh-5 canisters, but this does not seem to have been a common practice. This practice was in any event made redundant when the TDA built-in smoke generating system was introduced during production and retrofitted to earlier tanks.

T-54 tanks were upgraded on an almost constant basis. Soviet practice was based on carrying out mid-life plant rebuilds to ensure a lifespan of up to 20 years, so around the 10-year mark the tanks were sent to specialized tank repair plants for upgrades and rebuilding. Nizhny Tagil switched over to the production of the T-55 tank – essentially a complete 'product improved' T-54 – in 1958, and as new systems were developed for the latter tank they were, where appropriate, also retrofitted to earlier T-54 tanks.

One of the first new tank systems to be introduced starting in 1960 was the OPVT tank underwater driving system, consisting of a one-way flapper valve for the exhaust port and a 4-metre-high snorkel that attached to the commander's hatch. Designated as the OPVT-54B, it was nearly identical to the OPVT-155 system used on the later T-55. Early models had a two-section tube carried on top of the auxiliary fuel tanks; later versions had a four-section tube carried on the left rear of the turret.

In 1961 the T-54 tank received new ammunition and sights, with upgraded scaling reticule inserts to use the new ammunition (ballistic table 32 to replace table 22). In 1962, a new cover was provided for the engine deck for use with the OPVT system, and in 1966 the OPVT covers were standardized with those then in use on the new T-62 tank. From 1964, both 7.62mm SGMT machine guns were replaced by the newer 7.62mm PKT type.

The T-54 was also later provided with the TDA built-in smoke apparatus system, which injected fuel into the exhaust manifold, producing as good a screen as the earlier smoke canisters.

There was of course a T-54BK command tank, which was developed in 1957 as the Obiekt 137KTs. This tank was accepted in 1958. It used the same tried and tested R-112/R-113/R-120 radio installation but also was fitted with the 'Tsiklon' gun stabilizer system.

The T-54 series was one of the few Soviet tank designs that was licensed for foreign production, with the T-54A being authorized for assembly in Poland and Czechoslovakia and later in the People's Republic of China. The Poles and Czechs basically only modified the Soviet-designed T-54 to simplify production and add later improvements; however, the Chinese started with a modified tank as their Type 59 and then successively modified it into the Type 69, Type 79, Type 80 and Type 88 designs. Overall, if including later T-55 and T-62 production in addition to the T-54, more than 100,000 tanks were built worldwide based on Morozov's original design concept for what would later become known as the Main Battle Tank.

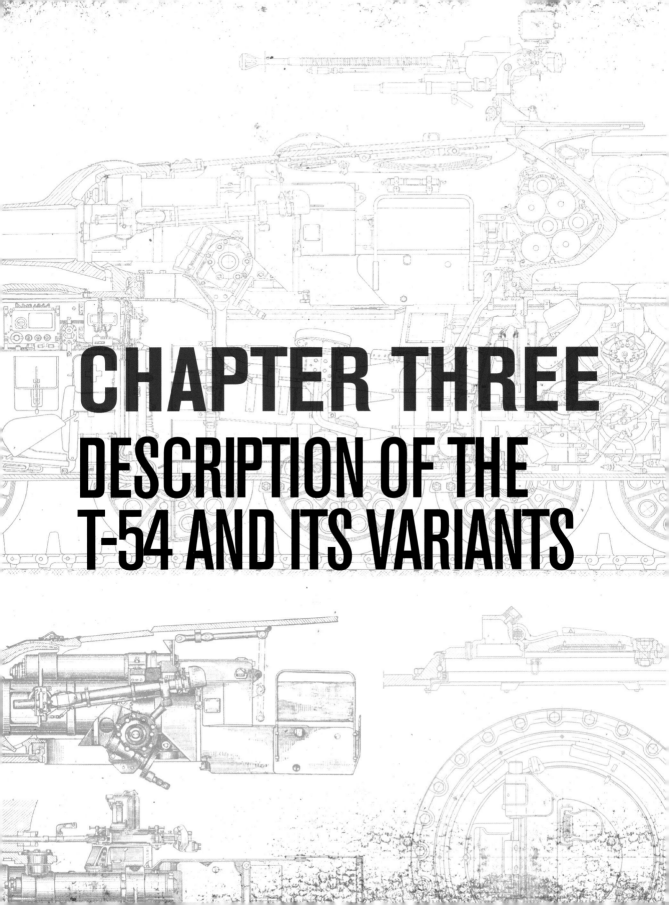

# CHAPTER THREE
## DESCRIPTION OF THE T-54 AND ITS VARIANTS

# T-54 MODEL 1945 (FIRST PROTOTYPE)

Originally called either the T-44-100 or T-44B, this tank was basically a T-44 hull with a new turret installed to house the 100mm D-10T gun. As such, it was based strictly on the production version of the final T-44 model (T-44A).

The tank was divided into three distinct sections: control compartment, with the driver-mechanic seated on the left, the storage batteries for the electrical system, and racks for 20 rounds of ammunition on the right side; the fighting compartment, with the turret and more ammunition stowage; and the engine-transmission compartment (MTO), housing the engine, transfer case, transmission, final drives, radiator, oil cooler, transmission cooler, air cleaner, and fuel and oil tanks. Other than resetting the ammunition storage for the 100mm rounds, there was little change made in the internal arrangements of the tank as compared with the T-44. There was no turret basket or turret floor for the three men in the turret crew.

The engine was a modified V-2, designated the V-2-44, producing 520hp and driving the five-speed transmission via the 'guitara' transfer case. The running gear was based on band brakes fitted to the final drives and used the six-roller drive sprockets from the T-34 as used on the T-44, with the two-section 500mm wide tracks also being from the T-34 – one with a large tooth to engage the rollers, one flat plate. The gearbox was synchronized from second to fifth gear. Controls were mechanical with servo boosters.

The suspension used no shock absorbers and consisted of torsion bars on all five road-wheel stations. Stations 1 to 4 were trailing link and Station 5 was a leading link; this quirk remained in use throughout T-54, T-55 and T-62 tank production. There was a greater separation between the first and second road wheels on all of the T-54 and T-55 series tanks; this was in order to distribute the weight of the turret over the middle section of the chassis.

The 100mm D-10T gun was provided with a TSh-19 telescopic sight for use with the main armament, with a coaxial 7.62mm SG-43 machine gun mounted to the right of the gun. A 12.7mm DShKM machine gun was mounted on a fixed pedestal on the roof of the turret between the loader's hatch and

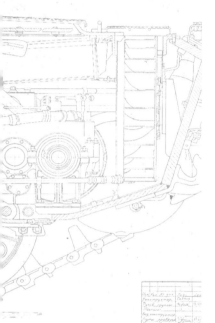

commander's cupola. Two more SG-43 machine guns were mounted as 'wing' guns on the track guards immediately behind the rounded frontal mud-guards, and were remotely fired by the driver-mechanic. Total main gun ammunition carried was 34 rounds of 100mm and 3,000 rounds of 7.62mm.

As it was based on the T-44 hull, this early tank had a 90mm upper glacis plate set at 60° from vertical and a 60mm lower one set at 45°. Side armour protection was 45mm set at 90° and the rest of the hull armour was 10–15mm; the rear plate was 40mm at 90°. The turret was similar to the protection offered by the T-44, albeit larger: 120mm frontal armour basis and 90mm side protection.

## T-54 MODEL 1946 (3RD–6TH PROTOTYPES)

Based on the findings of the testing of the first two T-54 prototypes, a large number of items had to be modified to meet state requirements. First and foremost was the elimination of the T-34 style track drive as it was judged to be obsolete. The new track drive saw the introduction of a toothed drive sprocket with 13 teeth and new cast tracks with notches for engaging with the drive sprocket, as with most other tracked drive systems. This was the final part of the original Christie suspension and track drive system used by the Soviets in the post-war era to be dropped.

The new track links were cast from manganese (Hadfield) steel and were 500mm wide with a pitch of 137mm, which was referred to in the Soviet Union as tight-pitched (mel'kozventchaniye). There were 91 links per side; 45 fitted with guide teeth and 46 without. The engagement notches for the drive sprockets were on the ends of the tracks, similar to the ones that would be adopted 20 years later with the new RMSh track links fitted to the T-72 and thereafter retrofitted to all earlier tanks.

The hull was up-armoured and also saw some design changes. The new upper glacis plate was 120mm thick set at 60° from vertical, but the lower glacis plate was now also 120mm set at 55° from vertical. The hull sides were increased to 90mm at 0° and the centre rear plate was now set at 45mm at 17°. The cast turret armour was now increased to 200mm frontal protection and 165mm side protection at varied angles. The additional armour increased the combat weight of the new tank to 39.15 metric tonnes, which was well above what the Soviet Army considered desirable for a medium tank.

Almost all of the other elements of the T-54 Model 1945 prototypes were retained; however, prototypes 3 and 4 were fitted with the experimental

100mm LB-1 gun with a small muzzle brake. Ultimately, the 100mm D-10T was judged superior and was retained for the life of the T-54 series.

As mentioned previously, Colonel Kulchitsky's evaluation committee had noted a number of deficiencies with the T-54 Model 1946 prototypes and, in addition to requiring a reduction in combat weight, recommended new steering mechanisms, a rotating floor (basket) for the turret, newer design vision devices, and shock absorbers for the running gear. The committee also found that the bearings in the 'guitara' and transmission and the torsion bars tended to fail prematurely and needed re-design and replacement.

# T-54 MODEL 1947 (FIRST PRODUCTION VARIANT)

The T-54 Model 1947 finally eliminated most of the bugs out of the T-54 design but it still had many unresolved issues. Even though the turret was re-designed to provide more protection over the frontal aspects and the side profile was lowered, the tank retained the 'zaman' (shot trap) all around the lower edge of the turret. TsNII-48 refused to give its full blessing to the new tank and noted that the institute was going to do research to come up with a superior design. The tank was heavier than the design specification at over 36 metric tonnes in combat order.

The armour protection remained 120mm on the glacis, but the sides were reduced to 80mm thickness. The cast turret now had 200mm frontal protection and 160–125mm on the sides depending on the location due to the casting profile. The weight was, however, decreased to 34.9 metric tonnes.

Side view of a T-54 Model 1947 with all standard equipment in place.

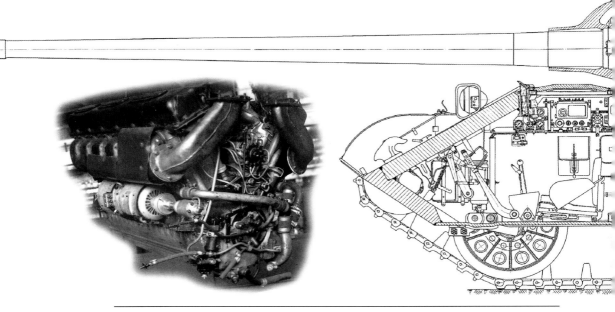

**ABOVE LEFT** The Vnbh54 diesel engine, showing the welded exhaust manifolds that connect to the outer exhaust port.

**ABOVE RIGHT** A side view cutaway of the T-54 Model 1947, showing internal layout and stowage arrangements. Note how the gunner's seat is attached to the D-10 gun.

**RIGHT** Hull assembly blueprint of the T-54 Model 1947, showing the fixed floor layout and T-44 style suspension mounts with no shock absorbers.

**ABOVE** The V-54 diesel engine, showing the welded exhaust manifolds that connect to the outer exhaust port.

**BOTTOM** A Soviet schematic of the engine/drivetrain layout, showing how the 'guitara' transfer case is fitted into the hull and provides power to the 5-speed transmission. It also shows the direct drive for the fan taken via the transmission.

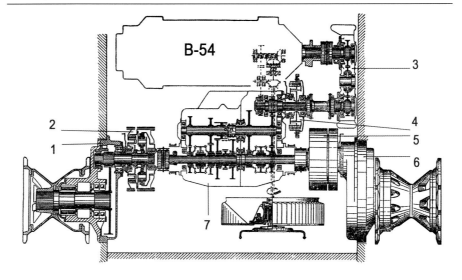

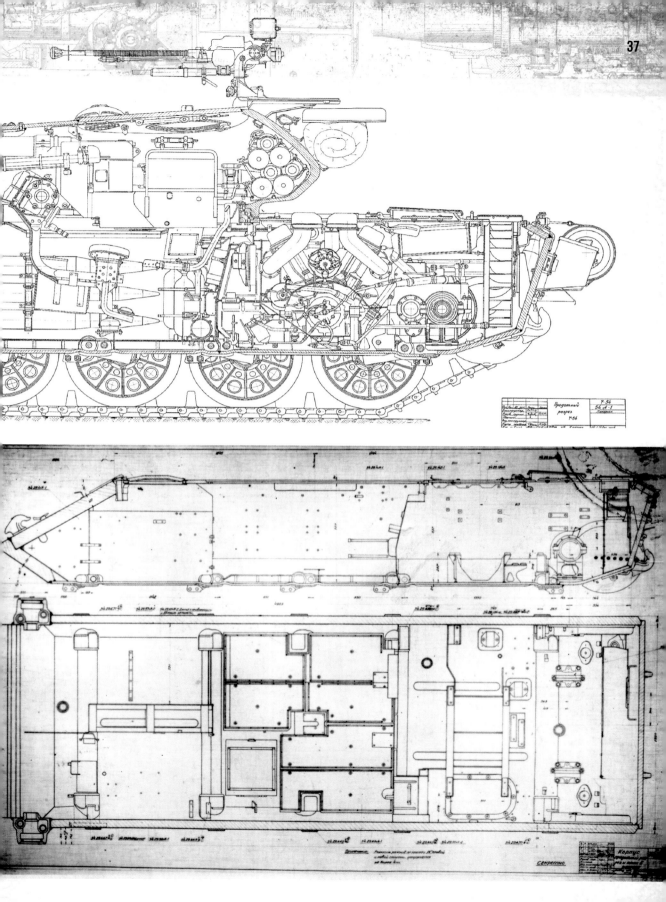

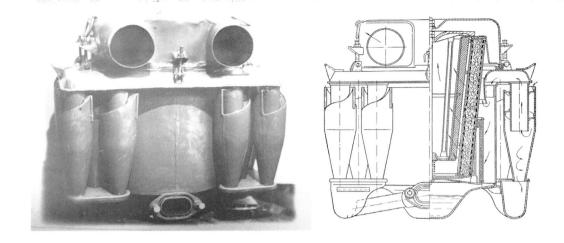

**ABOVE** The 'Tsiklon' type air cleaner for the engine, showing how the dust extractors feed into the catch bin.

**BELOW** The hull floor of the T-54 Model 1947, showing the original escape hatch location.

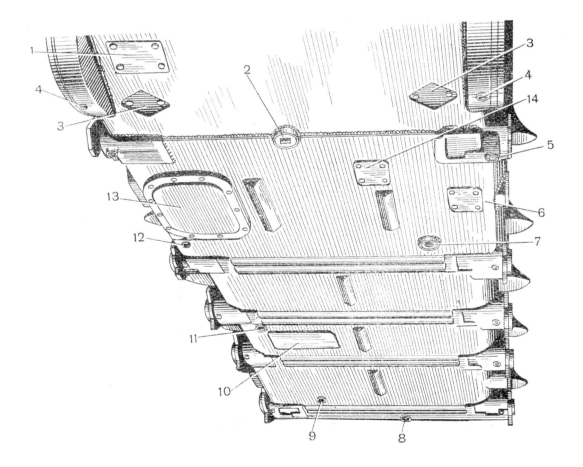

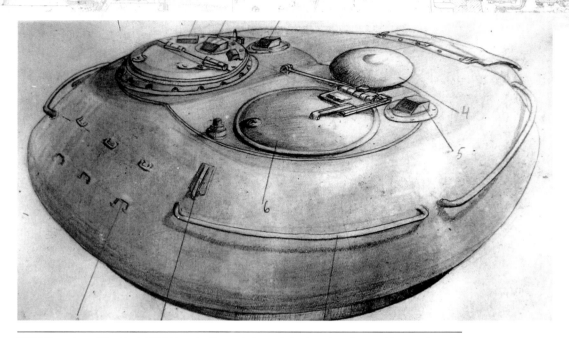

**ABOVE** Rear view of the Model 1947 turret with most elements in place, less the machine-gun tourelle ring.
**BELOW** The early 500mm-wide OMSh links used on the T-54 Model 1947. Later upgrades to the early tanks usually included the full production 580mm tracks, idlers and driver sprockets.

ABOVE LEFT A T-54 Model 1949 on winter exercises.
ABOVE RIGHT Rear view of a fully stowed tank with all fuel canisters, smoke canisters, and all stowage and ZIP bins in place. The tanks used the T-44 style 60-litre auxiliary fuel canisters with two per side for a total of 240 litres of fuel.
BELOW A T-54 Model 1947 after later capital rebuild. The tank now has three 95-litre fuel tanks and 200-litre auxiliary fuel tanks, IR headlights on the hull and turret side, and 'starfish' wheels with 580mm OMSh tracks.
BOTTOM The series production version of the T-54 Model 1947 with all equipment in place, less the BDSh-5 smoke canisters.

The 12.7mm DShKM machine gun was now given a rotating tourelle ring that swung away when not in use, similar to the mounts used on the IS-3 and IS-4 heavy tanks.

Internal fuel capacity was 530 litres, with another 180 litres located in three 60-litre cylindrical auxiliary tanks identical to those used on the T-44. These still had to be pumped into the main fuel tanks as required, but extended range to 360–400km.

The suspension now featured four lever-type shock absorbers on the first and fifth road wheel stations on each side of the tank. This helped reduce pitching and bouncing when moving across uneven ground.

The V-54 engine was an improved version of the V-2-44 and now provided with a pre-heater under the oil pan for use in cold weather starting. This used burning fuel to create steam heat to warm the engine block and engine oil in very cold temperatures.

The transmission now used twin final drive units for steering versus the old band brake skid-steering system, which resulted in much smoother movement of the tank. Maximum speed on roads was now 48km/h.

**BELOW RIGHT** Rear view showing the early location of the unditching log on the right track guard and also the large stowage bin between the two BDSh-5 smoke canisters. The storage tarpaulin is in its stowed position on the rear of the turret.

**BELOW LEFT** Front view of a T-54 Model 1947, showing the single clear headlight on that version. The identical nature of the two wing machine gun mounts can also be seen, with the left gun offset to the outside and the right one to the inside.

**BOTTOM** Side view of a fully stowed T-54 Model 1947 tank. The travel position of the AA MG mount, with the mount swung to the rear and the DShK machine gun facing forward, is clearly seen in this photo.

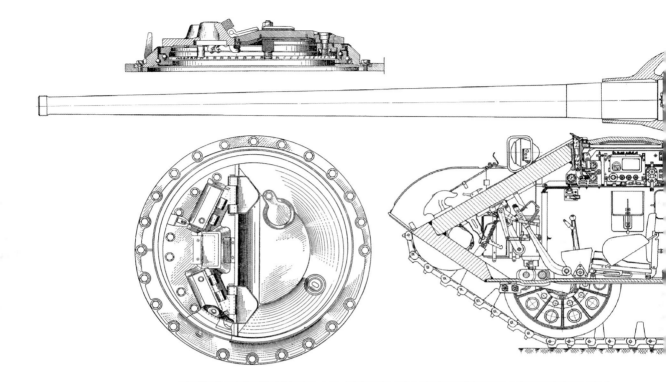

**ABOVE RIGHT** Cutaway of a T-54 Model 1947 tank with all internal equipment and ammunition stowed. Unlike earlier 85mm gun-armed tanks, all ammunition is now stowed in racks and not in two round cases.

**ABOVE** The T-54 Model 1947's commander's cupola without the rear viewing device that was later added to the tank. The small port is for signal flags or flares.

**BELOW LEFT** The upper hull of the T-54 Model 1947, showing the T-44 style round driver's hatch and three access hatch arrangement over the engine and air cleaner.

**BELOW RIGHT** Schematic of the operation of the MDK smoke canisters from the inside of the tank with the jettison pull toggles and fitting hooks highlighted.

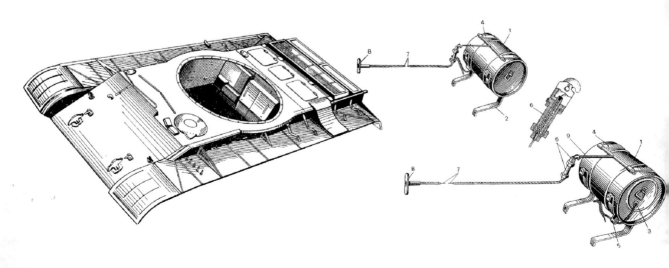

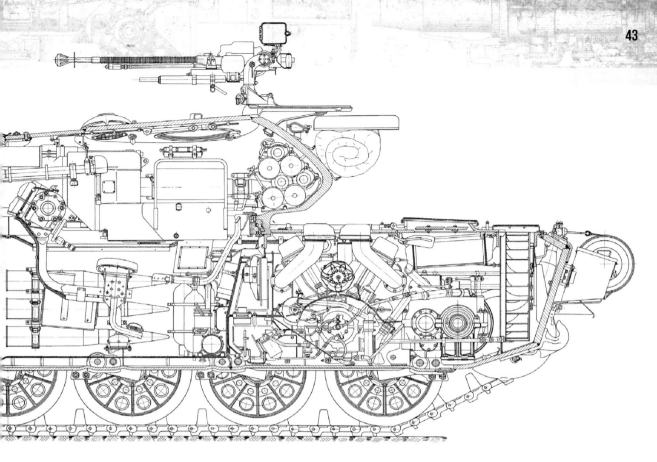

**ABOVE LEFT** A T-54 Model 1947 on test, showing its lateral slope crossing ability of around 30°.
**ABOVE** A T-54 Model 1947 showing its ability to descend a slope of around 30°.
**LEFT** A close-up view, showing the right 7.62mm wing machine gun mount and the ice cleats stowed in front of it. A total of ten cleats appears to be stowed in this arrangement, with the stowage mirrored on the left track guard.

TOP LEFT A T-54 Model 1947, showing its unprepared wading capability. 'Unprepared' is a bit of a misnomer, as the tank needed to be checked to ensure all drain plugs, access panels and seals were in place before attempting such a manoeuvre.

TOP RIGHT T-54 Model 1947 tank on winter exercise with the driver's foul weather hood erected and in place.

ABOVE LEFT The early model 12.7mm DShK tourelle ring is similar to that used on the IS-3 and IS-4 heavy tanks. This was quickly changed over to a built-in arrangement from the T-54 Model 1949.

ABOVE RIGHT Soviet manual drawing of a T-54 Model 1947 turret without armament or tourelle ring for the AAMG.

RIGHT The engine bay with the radiator and engine deck removed. Number 2 is the air cleaner and 6 is the oil cooler.

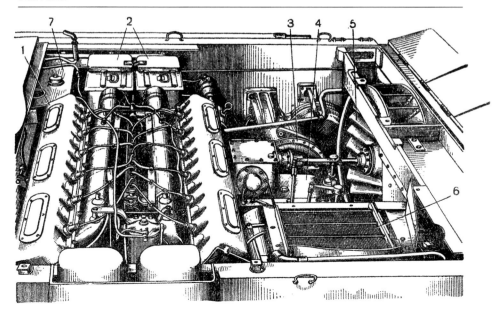

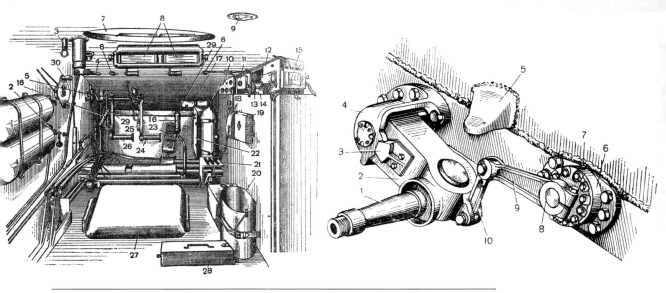

ABOVE LEFT The driver-mechanic's compartment in the T-54 Model 1947 with the seat back removed. The seat was adjustable only in the vertical axis.

ABOVE RIGHT The lever-action shock absorber installation mounted on wheel stations 1 and 5 on each side of the tank. Number 5 is the bump or jounce stop. The shock absorber was rotary in design, compressing hydraulic fluid to provide buffering.

BELOW A cutaway of the T-54 tank, showing the auxiliary cooling fan for the engine bay.

**TOP** The standardized driver-mechanic's foul weather hood and windshield. There were some modifications over the years, such as motorizing the wiper and heated elements in the glass, but the basic design never changed.

**ABOVE** The casing and installation of the wing guns. Each one had stowage for 500 rounds in two 250-round canisters but only one could be used at a time. The crewmen would have to manually replenish the expended one and clear the casing and links from the catch bag by exiting the tank.

**BELOW** An upgraded and rebuilt T-54 Model 1947 now fitted with 580mm OMSh tracks and 'Starfish' wheels as well as infrared driving lights on the glacis and turret for the driver. It also has the three 95-litre flat tanks on the right track guard and twin 200-litre auxiliary tanks at the rear. No wing guns are fitted.

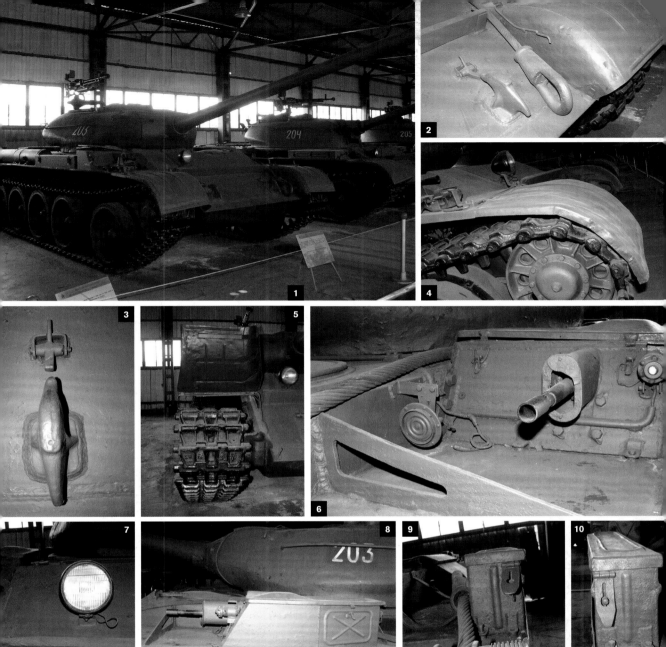

**(1)** The preserved T-54 Model 1947 tank at the NIIBT Kubinka Museum. This tank shows numerous repaints but is still in its original condition.

**(2)** Mudguard and tow cable thimble. Normally the tow cable head is clipped onto the tow hook.

**(3)** Close-up of the tow hook and locking clip on the glacis of the tank.

**(4)** Front right mudguard and idler wheel assembly. Note that the headlight is unprotected.

**(5)** Close-up of the 500mm RMSh track and the inside of the mudguard showing the reinforcing ribs.

**(6)** The left wing gun assembly with convoy light and the signal horn in front of it.

**(7)** The single headlight with its power wire exposed to the right.

**(8)** Side view of the left wing gun bin and the servicing panel at the rear.

**(9)** The tow-cable retaining mechanism.

**(10)** Stowage box and latch.

**(11)** The exhaust ports with some objects (wood blocks most likely) in them to prevent moisture and vermin from getting in. The ZIP bin lock is visible to the left.

**(12)** Rearmost ZIP bin with both locks intact.

**(13)** Mounts for what appears to be a later addition of an oil tank (now missing).

**(14)** Close-up of an intact lock and assembly. A hole in the blade permits a lock to be used in case of mistrust of fellow tankers!

**(15)** Rear engine deck area, showing the diamond pattern mesh on the radiator air intakes and exhaust vents.

**(16)** Rear left mudguard and support bracket, tail-light and power cable jacket, and left BDSh-5 smoke canister rack.

**(17)** Close-up of the BDSh-5 rack and igniter wire.

**(18)** The tail-light missing its lens (similar to marker lights but with a red lens rather than translucent white). The quality of the weld bead is also apparent here.

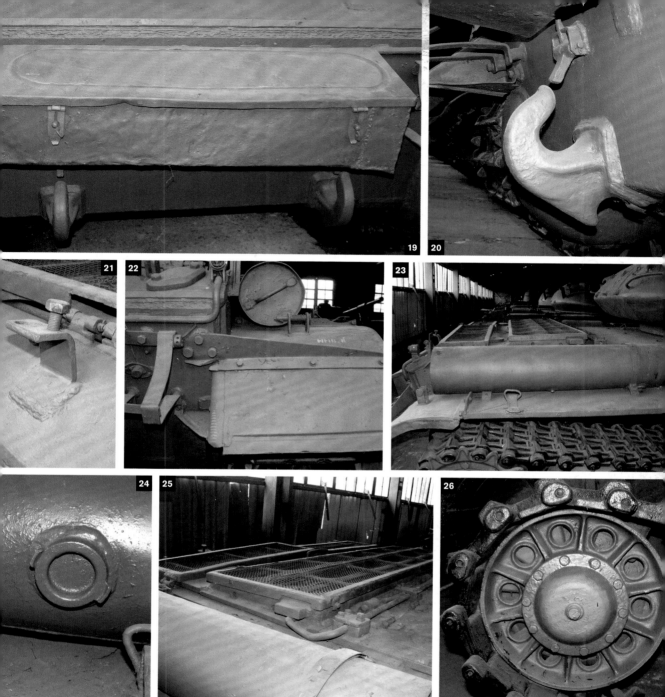

**(19)** The rear stowage bin as found only on the T-54 Model 1947.

**(20)** The rear and front tow hooks all had locking clasps.

**(21)** This appears to be a locking bolt for the winterization covers for the fan exhaust, but the cover itself is missing.

**(22)** Right mudguard and bracket assembly with tow cable clip visible in front of the fuel tank.

**(23)** The auxiliary fuel tank for the T-54 Model 1947 was similar to those used on the T-44 but slightly larger in capacity. It was not plumbed into the fuel system.

**(24)** Fuel filler cap for the auxiliary fuel tanks. Fuel had to be hand pumped out of them into the main internal tanks.

**(25)** Front view of the engine deck grilles with the heavy torsion spring for the engine and air cleaner access doors.

**(26)** The original T-54 Model 1947 tanks had a narrow solid cast idler at the front of each track run.

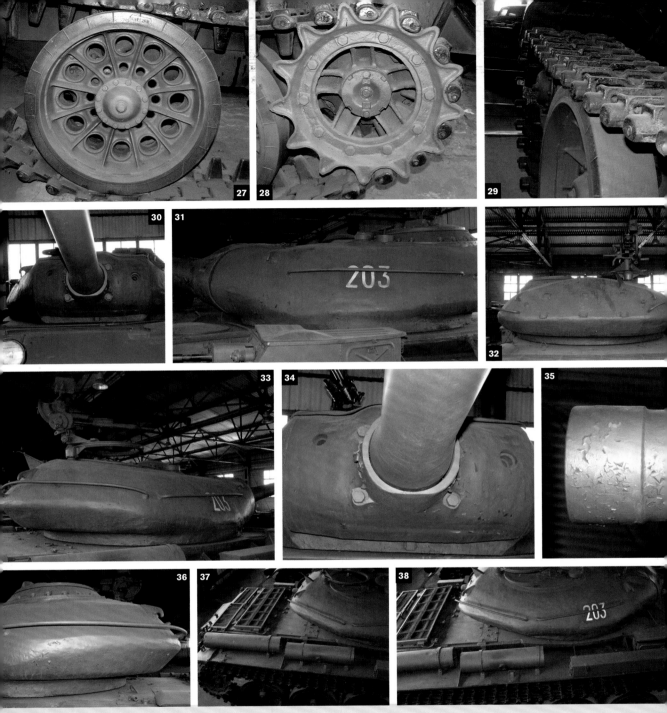

**(27)** The road wheels were nearly identical to those on late model T-34-85 tanks and T-44s.

**(28)** The original drive sprockets had a bolted-on 13-tooth drive ring and a five-spoke cast centre section. This design was kept for some time as they meshed with the later 580mm OMSh tracks as well as the 500mm version.

**(29)** The tracks apparently were supposed to just touch the number 3 road wheel when properly adjusted, so those on this tank are a bit slack.

**(30)** The original mantlet was approximately 1 metre wide and the design produced a noticeable shot trap underneath it.

**(31)** The T-54 Model 1947 turret was long and low compared with the others, but the lower surfaces presented vulnerable shot traps.

**(32)** The rear of the T-54 Model 1947 turret has a significant shot trap under it. VNII-100 and NII-48 both voiced concerns regarding this when the tank was adopted for service.

**(33)** The AAMG mount was particularly awkward on this tank and vulnerable to damage.

**(34)** Even though the mantlet changed on the tanks, they all used four bolt mountings.

**(35)** All of the early D-10T guns had a protective collar machined into the muzzle to provide extra strength. As noted, paint here is peeling due to lots of repaints without stripping.

**39**  **40**

**41**

**42**

**43**

**(36)** As with all later Soviet tanks, the T-54 Model 1947 was fitted with 'tank desant handrails', but these were much longer on this tank due to the turret design.

**(37)** An overview of the right rear quarter of the tank showing the two different length fuel tanks (the front one holds 60 litres).

**(38)** An overview of the right centre section of the tank with the ZIP bin and right wing gun in view.

**(39)** An overview of the right front section of the tank with the wing gun located on the track guard.

**(40)** A view of the complete radiator air intake and exhaust grille section of the tank with the substructure visible through the grillework.

**(41)** An overview of the left rear quarter of the tank, showing the racks for two missing 60-litre fuel tanks and the missing oil tank at the rear.

**(42)** The engine grille area again, but here the fuel filler cap covers can be seen between the radiator air intake and exhaust grilles.

**(43)** The commander's hatch is relatively simple – with an opening for a commander's sight, two wing viewers, and a port for using signal flags or flares.

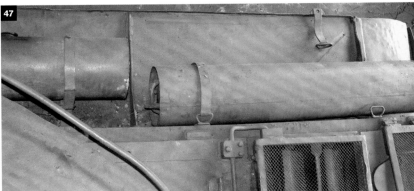

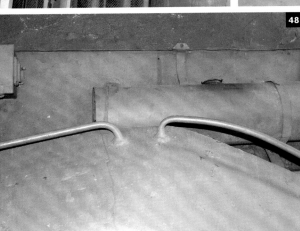

**(44)** A view looking down onto the left wing gun mount, showing the inner access panel to the weapon.

**(45)** Like the T-34 and T-44 before it, the first model of the T-54 used two broad louvres (*zhaluzi*) to control airflow to the radiator. The oil cooler was to the right in this photo and a 24-blade circular fan was under the grille to the left.

**(46)** The left rear wing area, showing the exhaust and the rack for the rear 60-litre fuel tank.

**(47)** Given that the long tank may be 80 litres in capacity, it would seem that the Model 1947 carried 200 litres (3 x 60 and 1 x 80) litres of auxiliary fuel supply.

**(48)** The long 'desant' hand rails covered most of the turret edges.

**(49)** A view of the right wing gun, showing the rear access panels to the ammunition supply (to the left) and the breech end (to the right) of the gun.

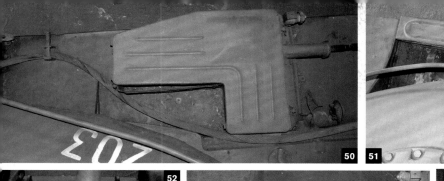

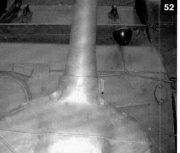

**(50)** Both of the wing gun boxes are identical.

**(51)** Right side amidships, showing how the tow cables were clipped into their mounts on the track guards.

**(52)** All three T-54 turrets – Model 1947, 1949 and 1951 – were asymmetric to the left to provide more room for the gunner.

**(53)** While the serial number of this vehicle is not available, it may have been one of the earlier ones, as this appears to have been set up for stowing T-34-style ice cleats on the front of the track guards (note weld spots). A single 500mm OMSh link is now located there.

**(54)** The entire right wing gun with the hatch closed for operation.

**(55)** The inside of the right wing machine gun bin (the left is the mirror image). It provides for two 250-round ammunition boxes, but only one feeds at a time, so the crew must leave the tank to reload manually and empty the fired casings and clips from the bin.

**(56)** Inboard section of the right track guard, showing the tow cable clip and the fastener and strap for a shovel.

**(57)** The 60-litre forward right tank, rotated 90° from its normal stowage position with the filler cap at the top.

**(58)** The 80-litre tank with one strap missing and the cap rotated downward.

**(59)** The mount for the left rear 60-litre tank with two sections of the straps missing.

**(60)** The iconic mushroom-shaped ventilator dome that is a signature of all T-54 tanks – and also found on Chinese Type 59 and 69 tanks. The loader's MK-4 viewer is located on the left of the dome.

**(61)** The 12.7mm DShKM machine gun on its mount with sight cover locked in place. Normally this is swung to the rear but here it is locked in the operating position (there is a plunger lock on the left side of the hatch visible here).

**(62)** The breech end of the DShKM. Note that it retains its ground sights as well as the anti-aircraft sight.

**(63)** The loader's hatch has to be open to swing the gun into position for him to use it; it would be impossible in this situation for him to do that.

**(64)** There are several braces for the AAMG mount to give it stability when in position (one is to the rear of the ventilator cover). Also visible are the gunner's MK-4 viewer in front of the commander's cupola and the J-shaped assist spring for the loader's hatch.

# T-54 MODEL 1949

The T-54 Model 1949 was the first truly 'standard' model of the T-54, and incorporated a large number of required improvements and changes that emerged as a result of early operational use of the first T-54 Model 1947 tanks.

The most visible change was the new turret design from TsNII-48, with a new hemispherical front section; the sculpted turret rear with its inherent shot trap remained, however. The mantlet aperture width was dramatically reduced from 1,000mm to 400mm and ports were provided for the new TSh-20 telescopic sight and SG-43 co-axial machine gun. This made a significant improvement in overall frontal protection as well as reducing some of the weight. Also, the DShKM machine gun now received a built-in tourelle that incorporated the loader's hatch, which rotated with the tourelle. This definitive mount would remain as part of the T-54, and variations of it would serve on the later model T-55 and T-62 tanks.

Weight reduction was a major factor in the re-design of the tank, and the new glacis plates were now only 100mm thick; they also were fitted together with a notched arrangement at the bow versus the butt-welded overlapping arrangement used on the T-54 Model 1947. This weight reduction was slightly offset by the introduction of the definitive new OMSh cast track links that would remain with the tank and the later T-55 well into the 1960s. These tracks used open hinge cast track links with pins, but were now 580mm wide, with the drive sprocket teeth engaging openings on both sides rather than notches within the links. All of the links in this track had guide teeth.

A standard production T-54 Model 1949.

**BELOW RIGHT** A cutaway of the T-54 Model 1949, showing the new turret front and the changes to the internal arrangements, such as the single bow machine gun replacing the two wing machine guns.
**BELOW** Side view of a T-54 Model 1949 in standard service configuration.

**ABOVE LEFT** A T-54 Model 1949 conducting wading trials.
**ABOVE** Rear view of the T-54 Model 1949 with all standard equipment in place with the exception of the undentiching log.
**LEFT** A command model of the T-54 Model 1949, showing its almost identical appearance to a T-54 line tank.

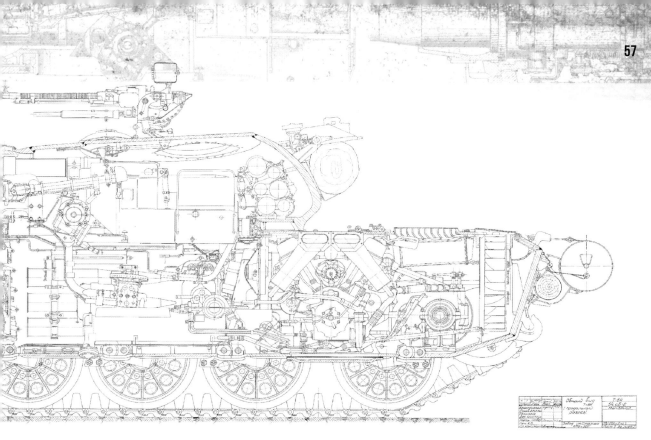

**ABOVE** Two T-54 Model 1949 tanks on exercise with white paint exercise markings applied to the turret rear. The numbers would indicate that they may be part of a tank division (3 – second regiment, 5 – third regiment).

**RIGHT** A T-54 Model 1949 on winter exercises.

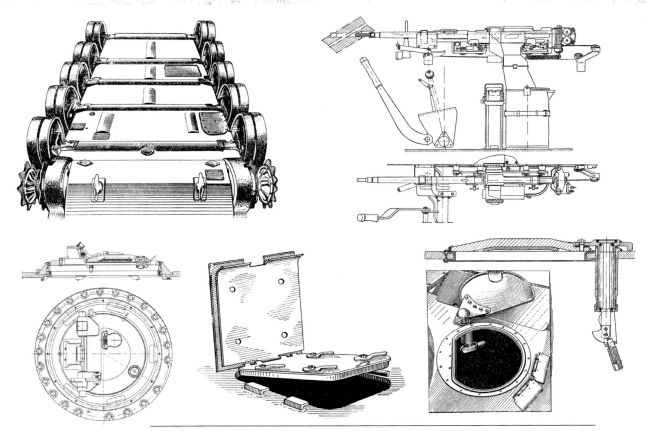

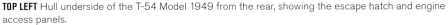

**TOP LEFT** Hull underside of the T-54 Model 1949 from the rear, showing the escape hatch and engine access panels.

**TOP RIGHT** The new location for the single SGMT bow machine gun next to the driver-mechanic, with its feed chute and catch bag.

**ABOVE LEFT** Plant drawing of the commander's cupola of the T-54 Model 1949 with all periscopes shown.

**ABOVE CENTRE** A drawing from the operator's manual of the hull floor escape hatch with the folding floor section above.

**ABOVE RIGHT** The evolving shape of the driver-mechanic's hatch, showing its truncated circular shape, which became the new standard. The hatch mount was later eliminated and the opening machined into the turret roof.

**LEFT** The original TSh-20 hinged telescopic sight for the D-10T gun, which was soon replaced by the TSh2-22.

**BELOW CENTRE** A generic Soviet drawing of the turret casting with some Model 1949 elements. The turret retained the undercut shot trap at the rear (not shown on this diagram) but eliminated the broad gun mantlet and improved the ballistic shape of the turret front.

**BELOW RIGHT** The hull of the T-54 Model 1949 devoid of fittings on the track guards and with a clean glacis. The SGMT port in the centre of the glacis is also not shown.

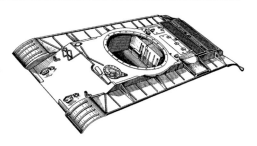

The commander's cupola was re-designed with removal of some of the MK-4 vision devices and installation of the TPK-1 commander's sight and a vision device for his observation of the battlefield.

There were external revisions to the track guards as well. The three cylindrical auxiliary fuel tanks were replaced by two flat 95-litre tanks on the right rear track guard.

Other improvements included changes to the PPO fire suppression system and a forced air heater for the engine block, replacing the steam heater of the T-54 Model 1947. The constant Achilles heel of Soviet diesel tank engines, the air cleaner, saw a new 'Multitsiklon' (multi-cyclone) design using an oil bath introduced for use in the latest tank revision. An improved main clutch was also installed in the engine bay.

The driver-mechanic's hatch changed from the round T-44 type design to a new truncated oval one that would also be a signature of the T-54 tank design. Also, the original twin 'wing' machine guns were now replaced by a single fixed SG-43 machine gun to the right of the driver-mechanic in his compartment, which fired forward through the glacis via a blast tube and a port in the glacis. The tank still retained an ammunition complement of 3,000 rounds of 7.62mm for its two machine guns and 200 rounds of 12.7mm for the DShKM.

An early T-54 Model 1949 with the new 580mm OMSh tracks and wide idlers at the front. There are now two flat 95-litre fuel tanks on the rear of the right track guard.

The older 10RT-26 radio sets were now upgraded to the 10RT-26Eh type, which provided clearer voice transmissions when used in radio-telephone mode. But they were still HF AM type sets with short range in voice and prone to weather disruption.

To give some perspective on the development changes undertaken as the T-54 design reached operational maturity, some 1,944 items were replaced on the T-54 M-1949, of which 857 were new parts.

**ABOVE LEFT** Rear view of a T-54 Model 1949 with the two BDSh-5 smoke canisters in place. There is no unditching log carried by this tank. Also note the covers for the oil cooler grille (left) and fan engine air exhaust grille (right), even though this tank is not equipped with the later OPVT system.

**ABOVE RIGHT** Side view of a Model 1949 showing the stowage of the tow cable and sharp undercut to the rear of the turret. The DShK is now mounted on an integral tourelle ring but is traversed forward.

**BELOW LEFT** Internal view of the turret of a T-54 Model 1949 from the operator's manual. The commander's sight is visible to the upper left, the gunner's sight to the right and below, the gun and recoil mechanism in the centre, and the co-axial SGMT to the right of the gun.

**BELOW RIGHT** Driver-mechanic's compartment of a T-54 Model 1949 tank with the seat back laid down for access from the fighting compartment. Air tanks for cold starting are to the left, with hatch mechanism, first aid kit, controls, and SGMT bow machine gun to the right.

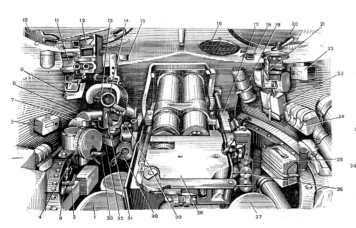 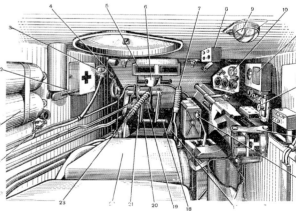

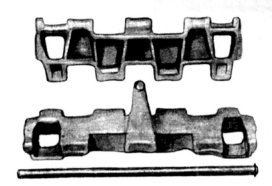

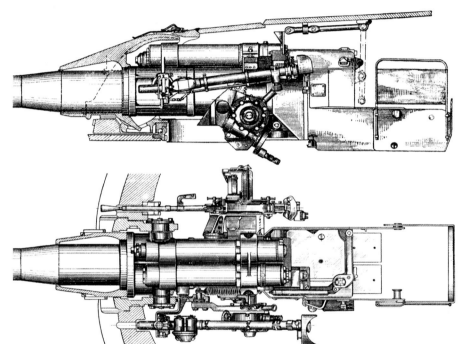

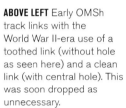

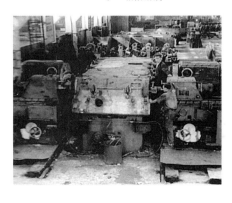

**ABOVE LEFT** Early OMSh track links with the World War II-era use of a toothed link (without hole as seen here) and a clean link (with central hole). This was soon dropped as unnecessary.

**ABOVE** The series production OMSh track link with a guide tooth on every link. These would be used up until the late 1969 gradual introduction of the RMSh rubber-bushed links, which were retrofitted to all T-54, T-55 and T-62 tanks as they underwent capital rebuild.

**LEFT** Cross-section of the gun installation in the Model 1949.

**BOTTOM LEFT** A T-54 Model 1949 hull under assembly at Nizhny Tagil. These men are machining the openings on the side of the hull, probably for the final drives.

**BOTTOM RIGHT** Rear view of a T-54K Model 1951 showing again how the command tank was nearly identical to the standard line tank.

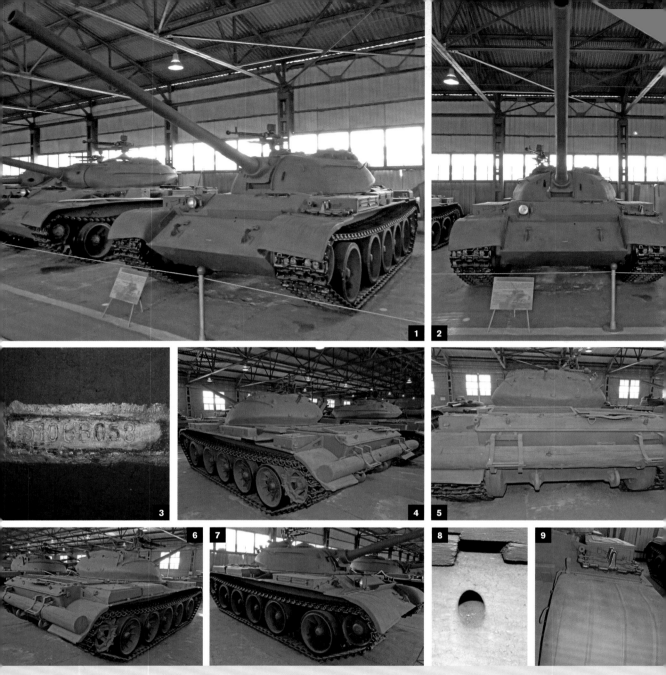

**(1)** The T-54 Model 1949 example in the collection of the NIIBT Museum at Kubinka. As with the T-54 Model 1947, this tank is nearly in its as-built condition.

**(2)** The 100mm gun is only 56 calibres in length, but as it is a slender weapon it looks much longer.

**(3)** The serial number on this tank – on the upper glacis next to the right mudguard – has been enhanced and is easily read. This tank, 5106V058, is a UVZ-built tank completed in June 1950.

**(4)** Rear view of the tank. This is the original rear plate area without the later rack mounts for the 200-litre auxiliary fuel tanks.

**(5)** Compared with other T-54 tanks the rear area is rather spartan, with just the BDSh-5 racks and the unditching log in its new location.

**(6)** The cylindrical fuel tanks are now gone and replaced by two flat 95-litre tanks on the right rear. These are now linked directly into the tank's fuel supply by piping, unlike the earlier tanks.

**(7)** The front wing now has a ZIP bin in place of the wing machine gun.

**(8)** The port for the single bow machine gun in the middle of the glacis. A blast tube leads back to the machine gun location.

**(9)** The mudguards are little different from those of the Model 1947. Twin OMSh links now sit on the front of the track guards.

**(10)** Left front view of the tank.

**(11)** The driver-mechanic's twin vision devices, which give him frontal and right aspect views of the terrain, with a blind spot on the left.

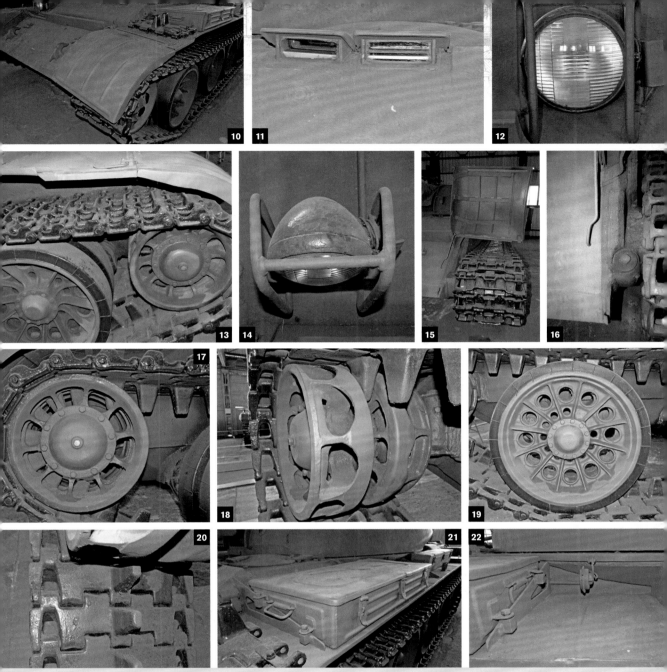

**(12)** The headlight is still a clear white light but now has a protective cage around it to prevent damage.

**(13)** The edges of the track guards and mud guards have bent edges to provide stiffness – the mud guard edges bend down, the track guard edges bend up.

**(14)** Top view of the headlight with the shielded power cable visible at the rear.

**(15)** The 580mm OMSh tracks, showing how they were simply widened by adding a stiffener and section to the older 500mm design. The drive sprocket teeth now engage the track holes rather than the edges.

**(16)** The track tensioner adjustment bolt, which moves the idler assembly forward to properly maintain track tension.

**(17)** The new design idler for the T-54 Model 1949. This is now wider to help prevent thrown tracks.

**(18)** The idler is a complex, lightweight and open casting.

**(19)** The road wheels on the early T-54 are actually about 15mm wider than the older T-34/T-44 version of the same wheel.

**(20)** The OMSh tracks are held together with loose pins inserted from the inside of the track and are held in place by a striker plate on the hull side that knocks errant pins back into place.

**(21)** The new large ZIP bin on the left front track guard. All the boxes were designed to be unbolted and replaced as needed, and have carry handles to permit easy removal.

**(22)** The area behind the bin, showing the turret race bulge and the location of the signal horn.

**(23)** Rear view of the signal horn, showing the power cable.

**(24)** Front view of the horn, showing its traditional Soviet design.

**(25)** Rear view of the front ZIP bin. This carried spare parts, tools and rags for cleaning the tank.

**(26)** Rear ZIP bin on the left track guard. This box carried the sectional rod and bore brush for cleaning the main gun. Also visible is the end clamp for the rear tow cable.

**(27)** The exhaust area with the reserve oil tank at the end of the track guard.

**(28)** The hold-down clamp for the rear tow cable, missing its spring-loaded locking pin. The sheet steel exhaust was easily bent and damaged.

**(29)** The oil tank, which holds about 12–15 litres of lubricant. This is a welded design but later versions would be pressed out of two sections.

**(30)** The mounting of the unditching log, above the mudguards on this tank. On later T-54 tanks the log was mounted under them.

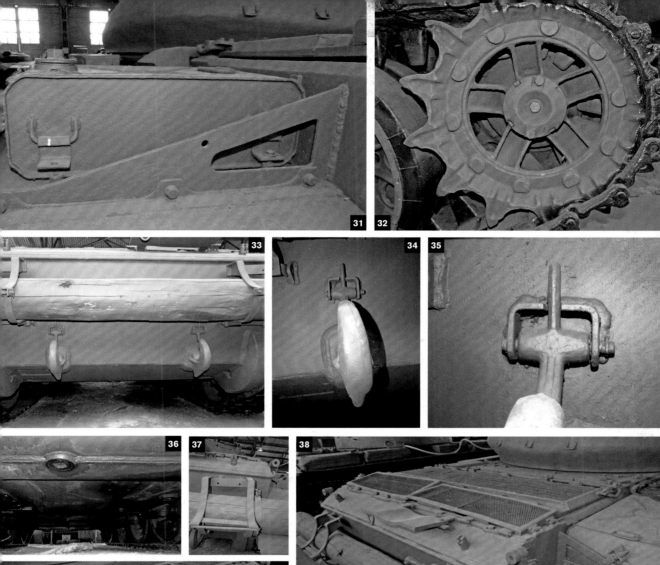

**(31)** The rear track guard bracket showing how it is welded to the hull but bolted to the track guard.

**(32)** The drive sprocket with its 13-tooth bolted ring. It is basically identical to that on the T-54 Model 1947 but now engages the holes in the track links rather than their edges.

**(33)** The tow hooks on the rear hull plate. Also visible below them are the inspection panels for the final drives.

**(34)** These tow hooks now have a new design of locking mechanism.

**(35)** A close-up of the spring-loaded locking mechanism for the tow hook.

**(36)** The tank hull floor from the rear. Visible here are the various drain and access panels to the engine and transmission as well as details of the suspension.

**(37)** The BDSh-5 racks are virtually identical to those on the T-54 Model 1947 but now sit above the unditching log.

**(38)** The rear of the engine deck area. Only one of the three folding covers is still on the tank (with the bulge for the fan visible).

**(39)** The post for fastening the left cover when open is visible on the left of the hull rear.

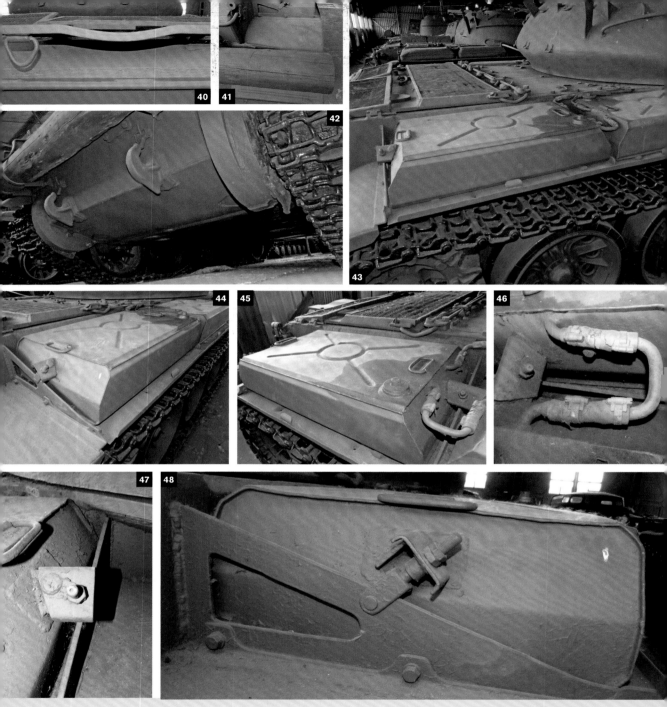

(40) The bulged cover for the fan section of the radiator exhaust grille. This was to prevent an air compression build-up when the cover was closed.

(41) This view shows the right rear track guard brace, the rear fuel tank and right-side tail-light.

(42) A view of the lower rear plate and final drive housings.

(43) The new twin fuel tanks on the right rear track guard. They are connected to each other and also into the tank's internal fuel supply.

(44) Each fuel tank consists of a bent sheet forming the body and two ends welded in place, plus connectors, brackets and a filler cap. They both have the traditional Russian 'Circle X' stiffener pattern pressed into them.

(45) Front view of a fuel tank showing the lifting handles and the filler cap.

(46) The connector between the two fuel tanks. The central hold-down is also visible.

(47) The hold-down on the front fuel tank.

(48) The hold-down on the rear fuel tank.

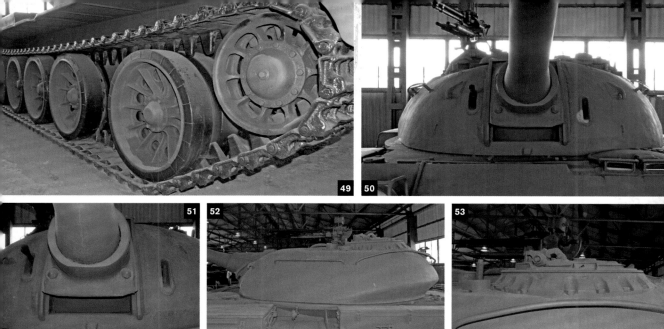

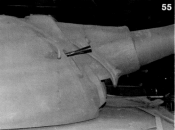

(49) The right side running gear. Per the operational manual, this track is nearly perfectly tensioned as it touches the third road wheel.

(50) The new narrow 'pig-snout' mantlet, sight and machine gun apertures were introduced on the new turret design.

(51) An armoured plate is located under the gun barrel to protect from splash when the gun is elevated to maximum limits.

(52) A side view of the new turret design, showing the improved frontal shape but retaining a potential shot trap at the rear.

(53) While the frontal 'desant' handrails are now more compact, the rear ones remain long due to the rear turret shape.

(54) The integrated AAMG cupola makes the right side more compact.

(55) The SGMT machine gun now has its own aperture and projects forward from the embrasure.

(56) Overview of the right side, showing the fuel tanks and the new large front right ZIP bin.

(57) Overview of the fuel tanks, showing how the fuel lines run into the tank and connect to the fuel system.

(58) Overview of the left side, showing the location of the ZIP bins, exhaust and oil tank.

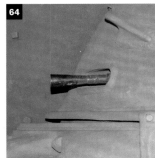

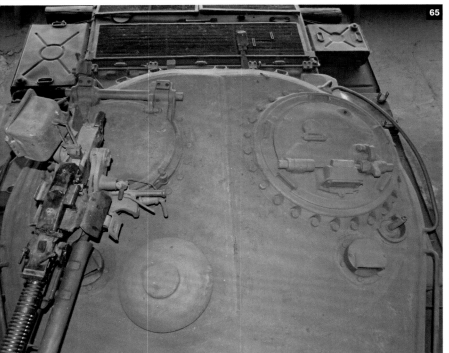

(59) The T-54 Model 1949 adopted a new intake to the radiator via nine fixed louvres with an element of armour protection versus the twin adjustable louvres on the T-54 Model 1947. The oil cooler and fan grilles remained unchanged.

(60) The new loader's hatch with the AAMG mount. The loader could now open his hatch with the gun mounted as it was fixed to the front of the ring mount.

(61) An overview of the DShKM machine gun on its new mount, with its AA sight covered.

(62) The engine deck area, with the twin heavy torsion bar springs for access to the radiator and transmission evident in the centre. This tank now has the stowage racks for the DShKM

machine gun when not mounted on its cupola.

(63) Top view of the forward fuel tank.

(64) Top view of the SGMT, showing how narrow the aperture is on the front of the turret. One of the cast lifting lugs welded to the turret is also visible.

(65) Overview of the turret roof, showing the MK-4 viewing devices, the ventilator, the radio antenna input and both hatches.

(66) The gunner's MK-4 viewing device and the radio antenna base for a 1-, 3- or 4-metre whip antenna.

(67) The commander's hatch in the open position. The only major change from that of the T-54 Model 1947 is the rear-facing viewing device seen here in the foreground.

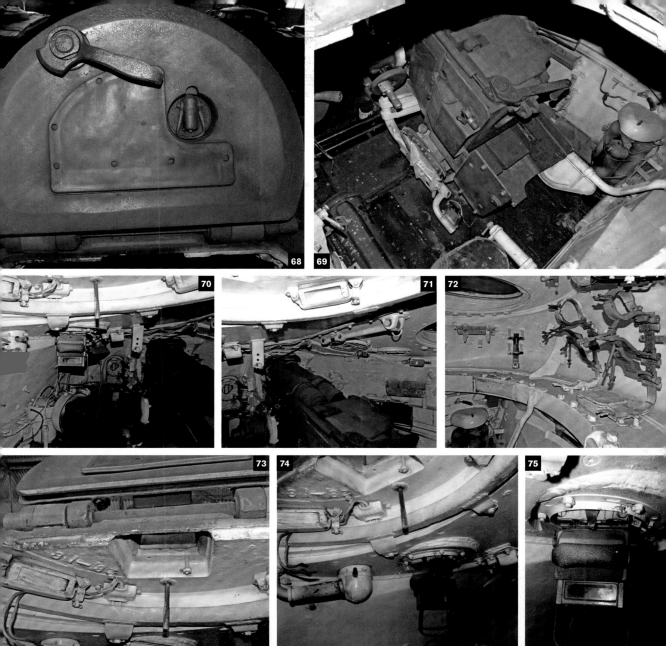

**(68)** The inside of the hatch with the hatch dog, 'headache' pad and opening for flags or flare gun use.

**(69)** The breech of the 100mm D-10T gun. Recoil guards were not a consideration when this tank entered service.

**(70)** The gunner's position in the Model 1949. The T2Sh-22 sight is missing.

**(71)** The interior of the turret with the internal gun travel lock in its retracted position to the right of the commander's cupola. In use it snaps loose and is connected to a mount on the gun breech with a push-pin to lock the gun at an approximately 5° elevation. The tank has no external travel lock.

**(72)** The turret rear, showing the ready rack for 100mm rounds and other fittings.

**(73)** The inside of the commander's cupola with the traversing lever in the centre. The sight/viewing device is missing.

**(74)** The gunner's MK-4 viewer from the inside. It can be moved back and forth for elevation and traversed for lateral observation.

**(75)** A close-up of the MK-4, showing the 'headache' forehead pad and control handle.

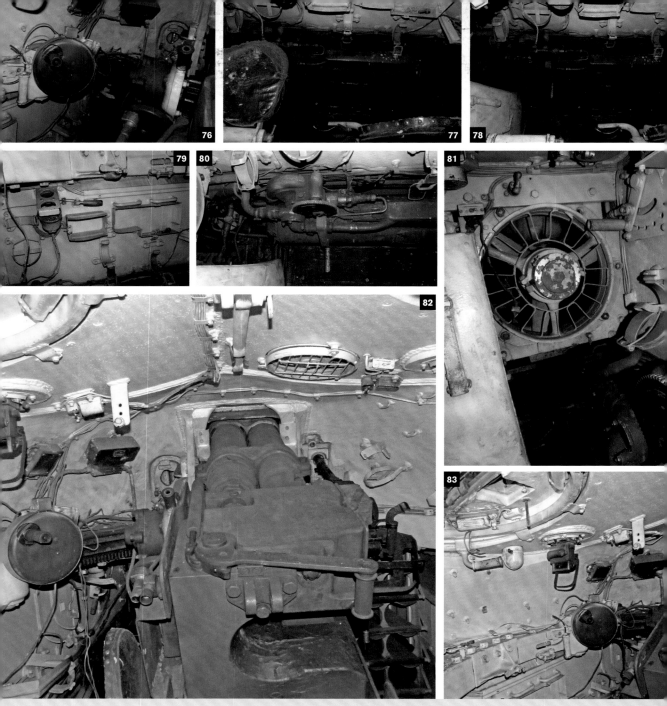

(76) The gunner's controls with the traverse wheel to the left and the elevation wheel straight ahead. The mount and closed port for the T2Sh-22 gun sight can be seen here. (77) The left side of the hull interior with the commander's seat folded down. (78) The left side interior with the seat folded up. The piping is part of the hydraulic system. (79) Brackets for stowage on the inside of the left inner hull. Stowed items would include spare prisms, fuses and storage boxes for delicate components. (80) The hand pump for the hydraulic system. (81) The air intake fan for the engine compartment that brings cooling air into the lower part of the engine bay and also helps clear the air in the fighting compartment. (82) The breech area of the gun viewed from

directly behind. The ears for the travel lock are visible under the activating lever. (83) Another view of the left side of the turret interior. (84) A view to the left of the turret. The base plate for the radio set (10-RT26 or later R-113) is visible in the centre on the edge of the turret race. (85) The breech block area of the gun, showing the cradle under the gun and the operating handle.

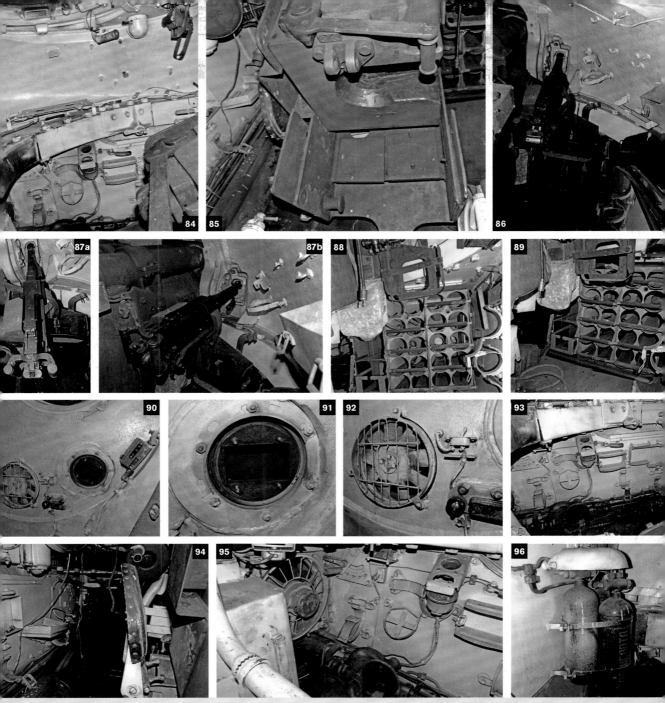

(86) The SGMT co-axial machine gun in place to the right of the main gun. (87a) The SGMT, though a 'T' (tank) version of the weapon, has standard spade handgrips as with the infantry model, but a re-designed trigger mechanism. (87b) Another view of the SGMT, with the ammunition rack for the gun visible here.
(88) The 'stellazh' ammunition rack, for 20 100mm rounds, to the right of the driver-mechanic. The rectangular rack to the left is for the storage batteries used in the electrical system. (89) Another view of the 'stellazh' rack, showing the SGMT ammunition catch bag for expended rounds and the ammunition rack for spare 250-round boxes for the machine gun. (90) Looking up at the turret roof with the turret ventilator to the left and the mount for the loader's MK-4 viewer to the right. (91) A close-up of the empty MK-4 mount. (92) A close-up of the turret ventilator fan. The controls are to the right and the wire runs outside the turret to the motor for the fan. (93) Another view of the stowage on the left side of the hull interior. (94) The gunner's seat is folded up to show the driver's position in the bow of the tank. There are a large number of cables, tubing and control rods running along the left lower corner of the hull. (95) A view of the left rear corner of the fighting compartment. (96) The PPO fire suppression equipment tanks (three 2-litre tanks filled with a mixture called '3.5') that could either be triggered by a fire or manually by the driver-mechanic

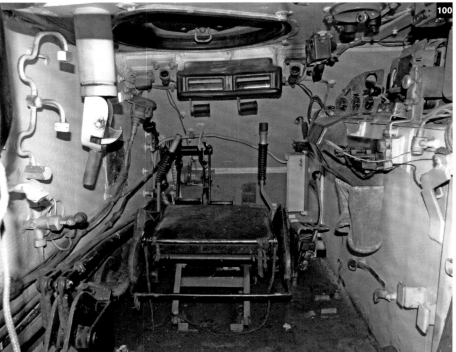

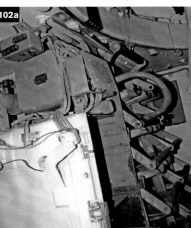

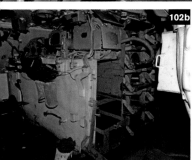

**(97)** The gunner's position, showing the long-range artillery-firing table fixed to the side of the gun mount. **(98)** The gunner and commander only had this short guard to protect them from the recoiling gun breech. **(99)** The gunner's traverse controls. Electric or manual could be used as required. **(100)** The driver-mechanic's position with the seat back lowered flat. This seat was fixed to the floor and it was only later that an adjustable mount was provided. **(101)** The left side behind the driver-mechanic's position, showing the wires and tubing running down the hull. Linkages included the control rods for steering the tank, shift linkage, and the throttle and clutch cables.

**(102a)** Side view, showing the flip-down locks to hold the 100mm rounds in the 'stellazh' rack. **(102b)** Right side of the driver-mechanic's position, showing the empty mount and fittings for the bow SGMT machine gun. **(103)** View of the driver-mechanic's viewing devices from the inside. They have a small amount of vertical adjustment via the two levers located underneath. **(104)** The driver-mechanic's forward right control panel. This indicates water and oil temperature, oil pressure, and engine hours used (gauge missing).

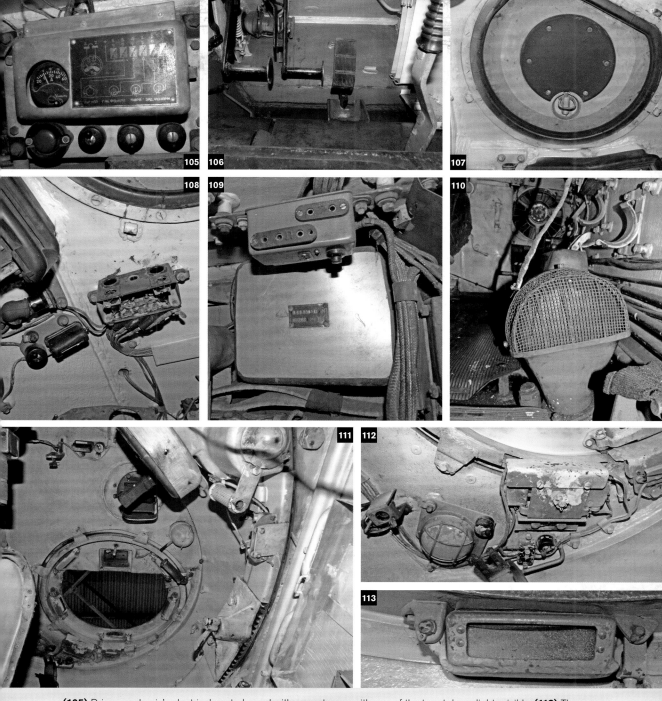

(105) Driver-mechanic's electrical control panel with ammeter, signal horn button, and light switches, as well as a schematic of the electrical system they control. (106) Driver-mechanic's foot controls – service brake, clutch, accelerator. (107) View of the underside of the driver-mechanic's hatch. The Model 1947 was circular; this one was truncated. The tube to the left is the hatch lift and traverse mechanism. (108) Part of the electrical controls for the tank, but missing some parts. (109) Part of the electrical power feed into the tank from the storage batteries. (110) Looking rearward from the driver-mechanic's seat. (111) View up towards the commander's cupola from the floor. (112) View of the area behind the commander's cupola with one of the turret dome lights visible. (113) The commander's rear viewing device (the prism is missing).

# T-54 MODEL 1951

The T-54 Model 1951 tank marked the definitive T-54 tank model. Even though changes were made to its internal fittings and equipment, very little was changed externally throughout the production run into 1958.

The armament saw a change from use of the 7.62mm SG-43 machine guns to the newer SGMT type in the same calibre. The TSh-20 telescopic sight was now replaced by the TSh2-22, with an upgraded reticule for newer ammunition types as well as other improvements. Ammunition for the SGMT guns was increased to 3,500 rounds of 7.62mm and that for the DShKM machine gun was increased from 200 to 500 rounds by means of six external mountings for 50-round ammunition boxes.

The biggest external improvement was the third and final turret re-design to a hemispherical design similar in shape to the cross-section of an egg. There were now no major shot traps anywhere around the circumference of the turret, and protection all around was increased: 200–108mm at the front, 160–86mm on the sides, and 65–48mm at the turret rear. The turret was now almost nearly completely cast, with only a pair of plates welded into the roof to support the hatches. The turret roof retained the distinctive 'mushroom' ventilator from the Model 1949.

The series production T-54 Model 1951 in standard service configuration.

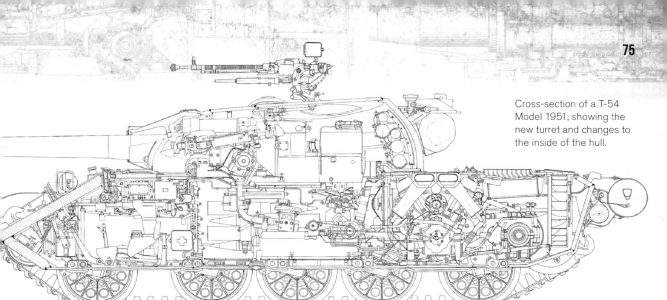

Cross-section of a T-54 Model 1951, showing the new turret and changes to the inside of the hull.

T-54 Model 1951 tanks on exercise. The lead tank appears to have just negotiated a small pond.

A T-54 model 1951 tank upgraded to 'B' standard during modernization in 1970s. Additionally, the tank got a KTD-1 laser range-finder in 1980s. It is from an unknown unit of the Soviet Army during the 'Kavkaz-85' wargames of the Transcaucasian Military District, Georgia, Summer 1985. (Andrey Aksenov)

Side view of a T-54 Model 1951 with all equipment in place except the fuel tanks and unditching log.

Fuel capacity was increased during the T-54 M1951 production run by the addition of a third 95-litre fuel tank mounted at the front of the right track guard. The fuel tanks were now made from two sections of pressed steel crimped and welded at the edges, replacing the multi-part fuel tanks mounted on the T-54 Model 1949. These tanks were also provided with fuel lines and plumbed into the fuel system so the crew did not have to manually refill the tanks. Also, while all tanks had been provided with rack mounts to carry two MDSh or later BDSh-5 smoke canisters at the rear of the hull, the T-54 Model 1951 eventually added fittings to attach a rack, firstly for a single

200-litre fuel drum and then for twin-200 litre fuel drums. This, along with other improvements to the driveline, eventually gave the tank a road range of around 650km. The tank also carried an oil tank containing 30 litres on the left rear track guard.

The tank was provided with a modified V-54-5 engine, still developing 520hp, but with some minor improvements and better fuel consumption. From November 1953, the engine was fitted with a ring-type internal heater called NOZh to improve cold weather starting. In 1954 the ring-type main cooling fan was changed from 18 blades to 24. One other change was that the radiator air intake changed from the T-34/44 style twin broad louvres to a series of narrow fixed louvres.

Some more sophisticated changes were made to the tank. A device called the EhMB-4 was added to the turret traverse mechanism; this prevented the turret from being swung over the driver-mechanic's hatch when it was open. In 1954 the turret was fitted with a rear headlight that was later used as a masked marker light, with red lenses or numbers for night operations.

Incidentally, the colour of paint used on Soviet tanks – 4BO green, which was introduced in the mid-1930s – was changed in 1953 during production of the T-54 Model 1951 to NPF-10 paint, a nitro-pentapthelene mixture that was marginally browner in shade than the previous 4BO green colour.

ABOVE The same tank as that on page 75 in close-up. The markings indicate it is likely the 6th Company commander, 2nd Battalion, of a tank regiment assigned to a motorized rifle division.
BELOW An upgraded T-54 Model 1951 now fitted with complete IR and night sight sets. This tank is fitted with the 12 brackets mounted for attaching engineer equipment.

**(1)** A relatively original T-54 Model 1951 formerly located at the Ordnance Museum in Aberdeen, Maryland, USA. The tank has some new fittings and also the 'starfish' wheels from a later re-build, but is otherwise as built. **(2)** The left side of the same tank, showing the toll of the elements. **(3)** Serial numbers give the year and month of production, the manufacturing plant and sequence number. This one – 5204E049 – indicates it was the 49th tank built in Kharkov in April 1952. **(4)** The tow hooks and latches are now relatively standardized. **(5)** Soviet tanks received a large number of checks and approvals before leaving the manufacturing plant, and many of them are seen here on the glacis. **(6a)** A stripped-down T-54 Model 1951, showing the glacis with the unique interlocking plates

and fittings for engineer equipment such as a mine trawl or bulldozer blade. **(6b)** Another T-54 Model 1951 glacis at the Central Armed Forces Museum in Moscow, with the original headlight and wooden splash-board in place. **(7)** A close-up of the 'pig snout' gun mantlet, with two of its four bolts visible. The frame is for a canvas cover, which is missing on this tank. **(8)** The guard and fittings for the later white light/infrared headlight assembly, with the latter missing. The brackets are for the splash-board. **(9)** The driver-mechanic's two viewing devices with their covers still in place. **(10)** The Israelis marked all of their captured vehicles with a number, using weld bead on the glacis and stern plates. This former Aberdeen-located tank was given 130443.

(11) The number was repeated under the splash-board on the right side. The other number (F15 203 MI) identifies that it was Foreign Military Vehicle number 15 belonging to the 203rd Military Intelligence Battalion (Technical Intelligence) at APG (Aberdeen Proving Grounds). (12) The APG tank still has most of its track guard fittings in place, such as the two spare track links and the forward 95-litre fuel tank. It also has a dilapidated but still present mantlet cover. (13a) The track links are held in place by being pinned to each other and having clamps hold the rear link in place. The attachments for the front end of the forward fuel tank can also be seen. (13b) The two rear tanks are plumbed into each other as well as the main fuel system of the tank, but the outer loop connections are missing. (14) All of the track guard fittings on the T-54 can be unbolted and removed for replacement or repair. This is the forward ZIP (tools, instruments, spares) bin on the left track guard, with more track link fittings visible. (15) This bin normally housed a manual fuel pump for either fuelling the vehicle or, if fitted with 200-litre auxiliary tanks, for pumping fuel into the main tanks. (16) The centre fuel tank, with the lines running to the forward fuel tank visible as well as the brackets for the tow cables. (17) The centre fitting between the two rear fuel tanks and the single attachment bolt. (18) The right rear tail-light and track guard with its brace. Apparently the last owners of this tank felt that one can never have enough spare track links!

**(19)** The left rear track guard and its braces. The rear ZIP bin is missing. **(20a)** The engine deck on the Aberdeen APG tank with a later fitting for OPVT equipment over the engine radiator air grilles. **(20b)** Another T-54 Model 1951 upgraded for OPVT equipment but with an earlier style of frame fitted to this tank. **(21)** The two rear grilles, with the fan on the right side of the tank and the oil cooler on the left. The former is missing its folding cover but the louvres for the latter can be seen through the grille. **(22)** The right rear section of the engine radiator air intake, showing the new louvres fitted to this model as well as the torsion springs to assist in opening the engine deck. **(23)** The air cleaner access hatch. The turret requires to be traversed 90° in order to open it and check or service the air cleaner. **(24)** The engine now also has a one-piece engine access hatch rather than the two smaller ones of the earlier models. **(25)** The modified exhaust outlet used on OPVT fitted tanks, with the frame to fit the 'flapper' valve to prevent water from flowing in and stalling the engine while underwater. **(26)** Another look at the fittings on the rear of the left front ZIP bin and also showing the placement of the signal horn. **(27)** The gun cleaning rod stowage case, showing how it bolts to the track guard rather than the brackets. **(28)** The drive sprocket with 13 teeth was standard for all of the wider OMSh tracks used on Models 1949 and later.

**(29)** The definitive idler wheel, which was scalloped to provide a wider area for the tracks to ride on, thereby preventing the tank throwing a track. This tank still has its original-style 'spider' wheels. **(30)** The turret also underwent numerous checks while under production and received checks as it went along the production line. **(31)** The rear markings placed on the tank by the Israelis. Note that this tank was re-fitted to carry twin 200-litre auxiliary fuel tanks at some point in its life. **(32)** This is a very early production T-54 Model 1951, with the welded oil tank and regular exhaust outlet. The former was replaced by a crimped tank similar in design to the 95-litre fuel tanks and the latter later received a heat shield and bracket to mount the OPVT flapper valve. **(33)** Overview of the early T-54 Model 1951 at the Central Armed Forces Museum, Moscow. **(34)** This tank also has the early welded 95-litre track guard fuel tanks. Note that both tow cables are also fitted to this tank.

**(35)** Not all T-54 Model 1951 tanks surviving as exhibits have fared well. This one in Mordovia has been stripped of all of its track guard fittings, and its infrared lights (retrofitted in an upgrade to near T-54B standards) are also missing.
**(36)** This tank was fitted with a full IR suite but the L-2 searchlight is gone, as are the headlights. The linkage from the gun mount to the later searchlight bracket is now also gone. **(37)** The tank shows it was upgraded to take OPVT equipment and is fitted with the exhaust heat shield, but retained the early tubular case for the gun barrel cleaning rods (the rear mount is still visible here). **(38)** The tank also is missing its mudguards. The cutaway for the tubular cleaning

rod case can be seen in the track guard bracket. **(39)** This tank has 'hedged bets', as it has both the mounts for the MDK smoke canisters as well as brackets for the 200-litre auxiliary fuel tanks. It also appears to have another MDK bracket on the right mudguard. **(40)** The APG tank has now been moved to the new armour and infantry museum at Fort Benning.

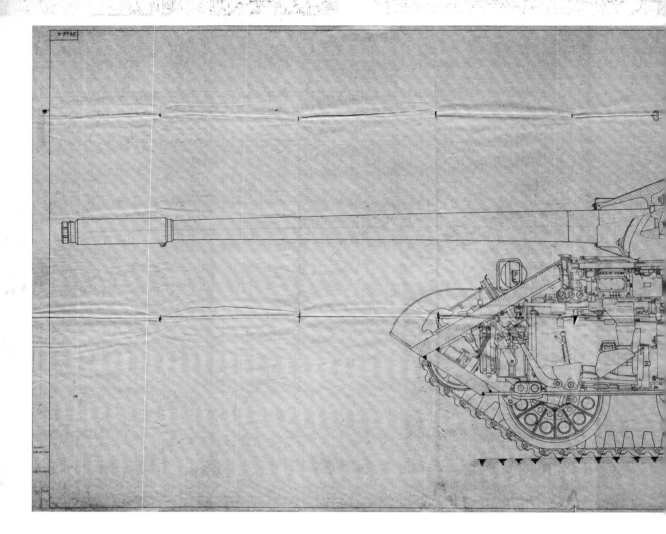

The T-54A differed little externally from the T-54 Model 1951 but was differentiated by the bore evacuator fitted to the new D-10TS gun. While the full production model blueprints show it with 'starfish' wheels, this one shows the original 'spider' wheels.

## T-54K COMMAND TANK (MODEL 1951)

While some 50 T-54 Model 1947 tanks were reportedly produced as command tanks, the first full production model command tank was the T-54K Model 1951. This was essentially a standard Model 1951 tank with a number of changes made, mostly to its electronic and communications fit. But unlike later command tanks, which went down to battalion level, these tanks were intended only for regimental or division commanders of tank units.

While the tanks retained their 10RT-26/10RT-26Eh radio sets for tank-to-tank communications, they were also fitted with an RSB-T or RSB-F-3T high-power radio set. This set was a modified aircraft set originally fitted to Sukhoi Su-2 light bombers and was a 50-watt HF AM set. Using a

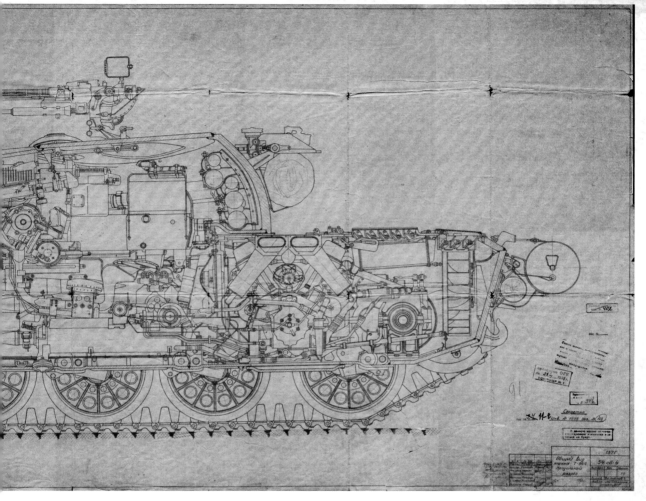

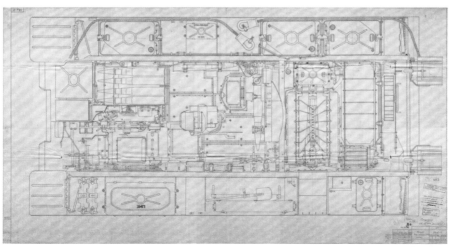

Plan internal view of the T-54A. The tank still has the basic original layout of the T-54 series, but with some changes to the stowage.

4-metre whip antenna, it had a range of 30km for voice and 60km for Morse code. A 10-metre antenna could also be used when stationary, which increased range to 75 and 150km respectively.

To power this set, the tank was fitted with a supplemental GSK-1500 generator set powered by a small L3/2 four-cycle petrol engine. Fifteen litres of fuel was provided for this generator, and as a result internal fuel for the main engine was reduced from 530 to 515 litres. To fit this equipment inside the tank – located in the right bow section of the tank, where storage had been provided for 20 100mm rounds – 13 rounds for the main armament and 2,500 rounds of 7.62mm were eliminated. The tank thus carried 21 100mm rounds but only 1,000 rounds of 7.62mm.

Overall, 215 T-54K command tanks were produced from 1951 to 1955.

## T-54A TANK

During World War II the Soviet Union received a large number of American M4 Sherman medium tanks, many of which came with a vertical axis gun stabilizer to help improve firing on the move. While many Soviet commanders had the system disconnected, as it was something they were not familiar with and not able to properly service, the concept was not lost on them and after the war the Soviet Union began conducting serious research into both single axis (vertical) and two axis (vertical-horizontal) gun stabilizers.

The relevant organization in charge of this was Central Research and Testing Institute (TsNII) No. 173, located in Kovrov. It worked on

Probable T-54A tanks upgraded to T-54B standards, with OPVT equipment on exercise. Note that the rear tank still retains its BDSh-5 smoke canister racks. The early two-section snorkel is attached to the top of the fuel drums.

hydraulic-electric designs and by 1952 these had shown enough promise that testing in tanks was possible. This was formally established via a Council of Ministers (SM SSSR) Resolution dated 14 April 1952. But by this time Morozov had returned to Kharkov, and in his stead the new chief designer at Nizhny Tagil, Leonid Kartsev, was tasked with the project of fitting gun stabilizers to the T-54 tank.

Plant No. 183 built two prototype tanks fitted with the single-axis 'Gorizont' stabilizer system during the second half of 1952, and after promising test results, Minister of Defence Bulganin on 21 October 1953 gave the order for Plant No. 183 to build an establishment lot of 50 tanks fitted with the new system. Now designated Article 137G, the tanks underwent range and service testing with success. On 22 March 1955, the tank was accepted for service with the Soviet Army as the T-54A medium tank. The usual three plants involved in T-54 series production built a total of 4,602 tanks between them from 1955 to 1957.

For the most part, the T-54A was analogous to the final production models of the earlier T-54. Externally the biggest difference between the two was the presence of a bore evacuator or fume extractor at the end of the 100mm D-10TG gun. Soviet tanks had always had some problems with what was called 'gasification' or propellant gases building up inside the turret and causing harm to the crew. The bore evacuator was basically a device with a series of holes drilled in the barrel of the gun, with a high-pressure cylindrical reservoir tank firmly attached around the barrel. When the gun was fired a projectile would build up a wave of high pressure in front of it as

Probable upgraded T-54A with the later IR searchlight mounting as fitted on upgraded tanks, and also the OPVT two-section snorkel mounted above the fuel tanks. This tank has also been fitted with the later 'starfish' wheel sets.

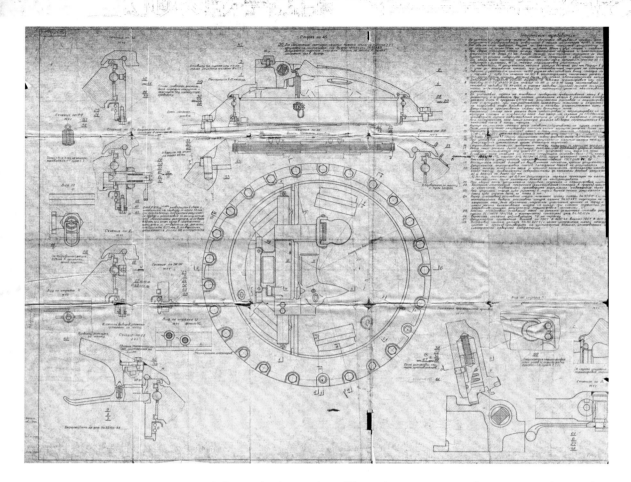

The cupola has been slightly modified and now features two rear-facing viewing blocks, giving the commander four plus a periscope.

it moved down the bore, thus filling the reservoir with compressed air. After the projectile passed by and exited the gun bore, the compressed air was released, forcing gases and burning propellant out of the muzzle of the gun. This proved a great aid in clearing the tank of propellant fumes. American tanks had been using such devices since the late 1940s and they were also added to NATO tanks in the early 1950s.

When the T-54 Model 1949 and Model 1951 tanks were in subsequent years rebuilt with stabilizer systems, if the gun was not worn out a muzzle counterweight was added to represent the weight of the bore evacuator so that the stabilizer would operate correctly. Worn out guns were replaced with the improved D-10T2S.

The tank was fitted with the STP-1 'Gorizont' single-axis vertical gun stabilizer system, which was a hydraulic-electric system using a gyroscope. It could stabilize the gun in the vertical axis over a range of 45 minutes to 3° 45 minutes with an accuracy approaching 1/1000 of range of engagement.

**ABOVE LEFT** The T-54A at Kubinka, showing it in as-built status without any IR fit.
**TOP RIGHT** The same tank, showing that it retains the 'spider' wheels of early production T-54 tanks. It now carries the crimped fuel tanks instead of the early-model welded ones.
**RIGHT CENTRE** A T-54A captured by the Israelis and sent to Aberdeen Proving Ground for evaluation. It is fitted with 'starfish' wheels and fittings for OPVT wading equipment.
**RIGHT LOWER** Rear view of the same tank. The only external giveaways as to where it came from are the two antenna mounts (next to the cupola and on the rear of the turret) for US VRC-12 series radio sets.

Traverse was either manual or electric via the TAEhN-3 'Voskhod' drive. Maximum traverse speed was 10° per second, and with the stabilizer on maximum elevation speed was 4.5° per second.

The gun was similar to the previous model but as noted had the new bore evacuator and the fittings for the stabilizer system. The gun sight was now the TSh2A-22, which had 3.5x and 7x adjustments. Maximum sighted range was 6,900 metres for the gun and 2,200 metres for the machine gun. (Effective range was considered to be approximately 1,550 metres, which is the point where the Soviet Army computed that 50 per cent of rounds fired would destroy the target.) Maximum rate of fire was 7 rounds per minute at the halt and 4 rounds per minute when moving with the stabilizer engaged.

The driver-mechanic was provided with a TVN-1 night driving device and the commander retained his TPK-1 periscopic sight. The driver-mechanic retained two vision devices (the centre one had to be removed to fit the TVN-1) and the rest of the vision devices were the standard MK-4 types.

Initially the tanks were fitted with racks for two BDSh-5 smoke canisters at the rear of the hull, but over the years they were also fitted to permit carrying first one, and then two, 200-litre fuel drums on the rear of the hull.

The radiator air intake louvre system was also modified. The fixed louvres of the T-54 Model 1951 were replaced with five adjustable louvres to better control airflow in cold weather.

During the production run of the T-54A, the 'spider' wheels that had been carried over from the T-44 were replaced with a new 'starfish' design that had entered production in April 1956. These had five broad 'spokes' rather than the 12 cast 'fins' of the original wheels and were also now fitted with wider rubber rims. While the road wheels remained 810mm in diameter, the new rubber rims were 165mm wide and gave a smoother ride. The tracks now only required 90 instead of 91 links per side.

New communications systems were also introduced on this tank – primarily the R-113 VHF FM radio set for tank-to-tank communications and the R-120 tank intercom system. The FM radio provided for clearer radio transmissions and less interference from natural phenomena.

The tank retained its use of storage batteries but the new ones now provided 140 amp hours (Ah) each.

## T-54AK COMMANDER'S TANK

As with the T-54K, the T-54A was also produced in a command tank variant, the T-54AK.

As with previous command tank incarnations, the T-54AK tank was based on a series production T-54A tank but with the necessary added components for command use. The tank used modernized radio sets, being fitted with the new R-113 VHF FM tank-to-tank set as well as an R-112 HF AM set for command use; both were plugged into the internal R-120 intercom and control system. The R-112 used fixed frequencies set 10kHz apart and was a much more stable radio than its predecessor. It provided communication of from 12 to 20km with standard antennas and at least 100km with the 10-metre antenna designed for use at the halt. But as it was a much smaller radio set, it only replaced five rounds of 100mm that were normally stowed in the turret and so the tank's operational endurance was almost identical to a line tank.

Fifty of these T-54AK tanks were built for regimental and division commanders.

# T-54B TANK

The T-54B was the final original production model of the T-54 tank, and it incorporated a number of new modifications and systems. Most important of these were the use of a two-axis 'Tsiklon' gun stabilizer and a night combat suite consisting of infrared lights, searchlights, and new dedicated night sights. Later, in conjunction with the development of the T-55 tank, the tank was also fitted with OPVT underwater driving equipment.

First and foremost the T-54B tank was fitted with the new STP-2 'Tsiklon' two-axis gun stabilizer which had been ordered by the Council of Ministers on 24 February 1955. As with the T-54A, the chief designer for the project was Leonid Kartsev. Three T-54B prototypes were built before the end of 1955, which were used for evaluation purposes. The new vehicle was designated Article 137G during testing, and the new gun was now designated the D-10-T2S. After design changes were made and testing completed, the tank was accepted for production and service with the Soviet Army by a Council of Ministers resolution dated 15 August 1956. The three main plants involved in T-54 production built a total of 1,628 T-54B tanks between them. Of these, 73 of the T-54B tanks built at Kharkov were fitted for the PST-54 flotation device.

**BOTTOM LEFT** The T-54B basically came in two versions – early and late. The main difference is that the late model was fitted with the OPVT-54 underwater driving equipment.

**BOTTOM RIGHT** Rear view of the same tank. While it has the original fixed searchlight mount, it is a late production model fitted with OPVT equipment, but with no snorkel stowed.

ABOVE LEFT Another T-54B of similar production, with the 'starfish' wheels as built.
ABOVE RIGHT An overhead view of what appears to be either a late T-54A or very early T-54B as it is not fitted with the IR sights, searchlights or OPVT system.
BELOW RIGHT This late T-54B is fitted with all standard kit with the exception of the snorkel.
BELOW LEFT A head-on view, showing the original searchlight mount fixed to the mantlet and the covers for the sight and machine gun, which are part of the OPVT deep wading fit.

T-54Bs and upgraded T-54As were shipped to many foreign clients, and these tanks are being uploaded for transfer.

**TOP LEFT** This tank is being offloaded on the other end, with a BTS recovery vehicle also sitting on the dock.

**ABOVE** All Soviet tanks were provided with fittings to lock them to the platform of railway flatcars for shipment. This photo shows a section of officers learning how to attach the lock to the tracks, which would then in turn be locked to the sides of the car to prevent movement.

**CENTRE** A preserved T-54B or upgraded T-54A with the later articulated IR searchlight mount and engineer equipment mountings on the glacis. A second (fixed) headlight was attached to the searchlight bracket.

**FAR LEFT** Side view of the IR searchlight mount, showing the linkage to the gun and the mount for the fixed headlight.

**LEFT** Another view of the IR searchlight mount and the gun mantlet cover, which is still in good condition on this tank.

**ABOVE** Rear view of the turret roof. Most of the components, such as the rear marker light and identification light, are missing.

**ABOVE RIGHT** The loader's hatch, showing its catches and brackets, and the mounting for the AAMG.

**RIGHT** Front view, showing the loader's MK-4 viewer and the power cable conduit for the searchlight.

The 'Tsiklon' was essentially two different stabilizers working together to give a completely stabilized firing position for the 100mm gun, and only required that the gunner hold his sight on the target; when the position of the gun matched the position of the crosshairs in the sight, the gun fired. Training speeds and stabilization speeds were similar to those of the T-54A. However, the stabilizer was not supposed to be used for more than four hours at a time to avoid overheating and damage. The gunner was also now given an azimuth indicator showing the turret position.

The T-54B was also the first of the T-54 series to finally be provided with a rotating floor for the turret to enable the loader to have an easier job of servicing the gun. It was not a basket but rather a rotating floor with electrical connections for the turret and fittings to permit it to rotate with the turret. Due to the location of the rotating turret floor, the emergency escape hatch in the hull floor was relocated.

The interior of the turret also received attention. The gunner was given a broader and more comfortable seat, the commander was given a guard to protect him from gun movement during recoil, and the loader had a folding seat attached to the turret race.

Early in the T-54B production cycle the commander received a new TPKU sight and vision device to replace the TPK-1. For night use with the new infrared system he had to replace it with the also new TKN-1 night sight. The commander also received a new OU-3 infrared searchlight for his cupola.

The driver-mechanic received a new TVN-2 device and a second headlight on the T-54B, now infrared, which was added to the glacis of the tank. The gunner received a new TPN-1 night sight to the left of his TSh2A-22 sight and mounted where his MK-4 vision device had previously been in the turret roof. Finally, a large L-2 infrared searchlight was located to the right and above the gun with a mount welded directly to the mantlet. It was only later, when new developments were made to the T-55 tank, that an improved mount linked to the gun, permitting it to elevate with the main gun barrel, was added. This installation was used to retrofit older T-54s dating back to and including the T-54 Model 1949. All remaining components of the T-54B were as for the T-54A.

Beginning in September 1957, the T-54B was also fitted with the OPVT-54 underwater driving system. This was to permit the tank to drive underwater to a depth of 5 metres and for a distance of no more than 700 metres, essentially to permit crossing the majority of rivers in Europe. The system consisted of fixed and attached components, most of which were permanently installed, such as seals for the occupied sections of the tank, an inflatable turret race seal, and mounts for a snorkel and exhaust flapper valve. There were rubber-impregnated covers for the gun muzzle, telescopic sight port, and co-axial machine gun as well as various forms of folding covers and seals for the engine bay. A 4-metre-long snorkel was attached in place of the loader's MK-4 viewer on the right side of the turret, and a flapper valve device bolted to the flange was fitted to the exhaust aperture on the left side of the hull. Finally, four closed gas masks and life jackets were provided for crew escape if the tank stalled or flooded on the bottom of a river.

**TOP LEFT** The driver-mechanic's hatch with retracted periscopes and the engineer equipment fittings on the left side of the glacis.

**TOP RIGHT** The oil tank, now mounted above the exhaust outlet above a heat shield and holding 20 litres of engine oil.

**ABOVE LEFT** The stowage bin for the main searchlight when not mounted, located behind the exhaust outlet on the left track guard. The dome to clear the rear of the light is obvious.

**ABOVE RIGHT** The engine deck of the T-54B with the early OPVT rack for attaching the covers over the radiator grilles.

**BELOW** Commander's cupola and IR night sight with protective cover bolted in place. The commander's IR searchlight is missing but the hole in the cupola for the control rod to the light is visible to the left of the periscope.

**ABOVE** The cover for the direct fire sight has a glass window, but a rubber seal was fitted for underwater driving.

**TOP LEFT** The co-axial machine gun was also fitted with a rubber cover, which is installed here, but is damaged.

**TOP RIGHT** Later T-54s were fitted with brackets on the turret rear to carry the 12.7mm DShKM machine gun when not in action. The mount plugged into the thumbscrew bracket, the gun rested on the mount, and the barrel was fitted into the clamp on the left. Later, racks for six 50-round ammunition canisters were fitted to the right side of the turret.

**ABOVE LEFT** The mount for the AAMG is still fitted to this tank. The small case covered the anti-aircraft sight. For ground targets the gun used its normal sights.

**ABOVE RIGHT** The mount had an elevating wheel on the right, with a lever and brake on the left to either free swivel the cupola or lock it in place. A trigger was fitted to the cable that ran to the firing mechanism of the gun on the handwheel.

Front view of the DShKM mount, showing how it tightened into the cupola.

A relatively intact T-54B located at the T-34 Museum at Sholkovo near Moscow, with the original searchlight bracket and most of the external fitments still in place.

**TOP LEFT** Front view of a T-54B at the T-34 Museum at Sholokovo, near Moscow, with an extra ZIP bin over the left track guard and the extended 200-litre fuel tank brackets to stow the two-piece OPVT snorkel. The unditching log is missing.
**TOP RIGHT** Rear view of the turret with the marker light, tie loops and AAMG stowage brackets all present.
**ABOVE** The rear hull plate with all of its brackets present, but the fuel tank racks, snorkel and unditching log all missing.
**ABOVE RIGHT** Front left mudguard area showing the 'spring' for keeping it in place and also the location of the port for the bow 7.62mm machine gun.
**RIGHT** Overview of a T-54B as preserved in a village west of Moscow.
**BOTTOM** Even with the change in wheels (the 'starfish' wheels being wider than the 'spider' wheels), the suspension geometry remained unchanged.

An improved version, the OPVT-54B, was introduced in April 1958 with better seals as well as a new rubberized rubber-impregnated canvas cover to be fitted over the radiator air intake at the rear of the tank (the exhaust section had folding metal covers).

The snorkel for all T-54B tanks (and later upgraded T-54 and T-54A tanks) consisted of two nesting sections roughly the width of the hull. The designers went through several different iterations to find out where to best stow them. One early version had them on the left side of the turret with about a metre of the sections sticking out and thus vulnerable to damage. The second location appears to have been on the engine deck, but the third one was more common, with the sections attached to brackets on top of the twin 200-litre auxiliary fuel tanks. The final version (most common on the upgraded tanks) used brackets on the stern plate above the unditching log and below the racks for the twin fuel tanks. The T-54 series does not seem to ever have been issued the later four-section snorkel that came into use around 1970.

Preserved T-54B tanks are a rather mixed lot, as many of them are missing one or more standard features of the tank. This tank has had its main searchlight removed.

## T-54BK COMMANDER'S TANK

As with the previous T-54 and T-54A tanks, the T-54B also received a dedicated command tank variant. In 1957–58 Plant No. 183 built 180 of these tanks.

The tank had the same communications fit as the T-54AK, namely the R-113 VHF FM set and the R-112 HF AM set with the R-120 intercom system and several antennas, including the standard 10-metre type used for static site operation. The generator set was now an AB-1-P/30 set powered by the L3/2 petrol engine. As with the T-54AK, the tank carried five fewer 100mm rounds to accommodate the command equipment.

## LATER MODIFICATIONS

Soviet doctrine laid out three distinct levels of tank servicing: Technical Inspection 1, Technical Inspection 2, and Capital Rebuild. The first two – called TO-1 and TO-2 in Russian – required major servicing of the tank at certain points in its life based on kilometres driven, hours of operation, and age. Regular servicing, as with all military vehicles, was the responsibility of the crew and unit during their operations of the tank.

Capital rebuild at specially designated tank repair plants (TRZs) in the USSR was something the Russians undertook seriously. Most armoured warfare experts determined the life of a tank in Soviet Army service to be approximately 20 years, and thus around the ten-year mark the tank was to be sent off to such plants for replacement of worn-out components and upgrading and standardization to the level of newer models where appropriate. This meant that many of the T-54 tanks from Model 1947 to T-54B were later upgraded with T-55 components and new equipment to nearly the same level as T-55 tanks then in series production.

The limitations on the upgrades were usually the physical model of tank being upgraded; for example, the Model 1947 was not seen as useful due to its obsolete turret design. As a result, the earliest series production T-54 was more likely to receive the mechanical upgrades but be converted into a BTS tank repair and recovery vehicle. The T-54 Model 1949 received many of the upgrades but does not appear to have received the OPVT deep wading equipment as standard.

The upgrades undertaken on the T-54 during capital repair included any or all of the following:

- New RMSh tracks and 'starfish' road wheels, later model drive sprockets and idler wheels;
- Infrared sights and night combat/driving equipment;
- Stabilizers (primarily the 'Tsiklon' version based on the start of capital rebuilding for the T-54 series tanks circa 1957–59): the key recognition feature on upgraded tanks would be the fitting of a counterweight to the muzzle of the older D-10T gun;
- Retrofit of R-113 radio sets and R-120 intercom systems, and later R-123 VHF FM radio sets;
- OPVT equipment for the T-54 Model 1951 and T-54A tanks;
- Racks for fitting twin 200-litre auxiliary fuel drums instead of the twin BDSh-5 smoke canisters (this was usually due to the later installation of T-55 engines fitted with the TDA internal smoke generating system): as built, these drums were not plumbed into the fuel system, but more recent changes can involve direct plumbing;
- Improved electronics (starters, generators, drive motors, etc.) for electrical components;
- Any other recent developments that could be used with overseas sale of what the Soviets later considered to have become second line tanks (laser range finders, side skirts, applique armour, etc.).

Many of these modernized and upgraded tanks were arbitrarily given new designations, such as T-54M, T-54AM, T-54BM, T-54KM, T-54AKM and T-54BKM.

Many T-54 Model 1949 and later tanks received a number of different upgrades prior to sale or supply to Soviet client states, and even today these T-54 tanks can still be found in service in some countries.

# CHAPTER FOUR
## DERIVATIVES OF THE T-54 TANK FAMILY

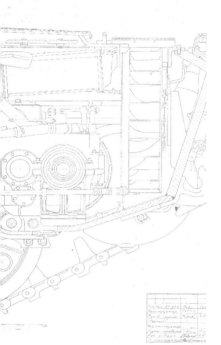

The T-54 tank chassis was used for several types of secondary roles: self-propelled guns, self-propelled anti-aircraft guns, bridge launchers, repair and recovery vehicles, and flamethrower tanks. Most of these were based on concepts developed in the late 1930s and used during World War II, with some proving to be better than others. A large number of prototypes and experimental tanks were also developed based on the T-54 tank chassis.

## SELF-PROPELLED GUNS

### SU-122-54 ASSAULT GUN

The Red Army made great use of assault guns during World War II for long-range tank killer roles and for close support against fortified targets, and that continued in the early post-war era. As the then 'wartime' T-44 was being developed, work was undertaken on a 122mm D-25S armed assault gun version in the late summer and autumn of 1944, the SU-122-44. But in late 1944 there was no perceived need for another such weapon on a medium tank chassis when the SU-100 medium and ISU-122 and ISU-152 heavy assault guns were in production and service.

The post-war Soviet Army returned to the theme, however. In 1948, research began on using the T-54 as the basis for a self-propelled 122mm assault gun fitted with either a D-25T or (from 1952) the new 122mm M-62S rifled gun. The project was tasked to Plant No. 174 in Omsk, with the chief designer being A. Eh. Sudin. The working drawings and sketches were developed by the summer of 1949, and a

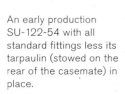

An early production SU-122-54 with all standard fittings less its tarpaulin (stowed on the rear of the casemate) in place.

**TOP LEFT** The preserved SU-122-54 at the Kubinka Tank Museum near Moscow. The trials prototype is virtually complete, with all of the main components intact.
**TOP RIGHT** A close-up of the gun mantlet with its co-axial 14.5mm KPVT machine gun and anti-aircraft weapon of the same type.
**ABOVE LEFT** Due to the casemate fighting compartment being towards the front end of the vehicle, the front three-wheel station locations were dissimilar from the T-54 to distribute the weight. Note the vehicle is now fitted with 'starfish' wheels, so probably went through capital rebuild.
**ABOVE RIGHT** This SU-122-54 mounts white light headlights in protective canisters on either side of the hull. The signal horn is on the right side with the radio whip antenna mount in front of it.

prototype model was built in December 1950. Now designated as Obiekt 600, the new assault gun underwent development and was approved for production, but in 1952 it was decided that a sufficient number of guns had to be built to provide an establishment lot for military service testing, for which purpose three more prototypes were built in July 1953. Further development of the 122mm M-62S gun option was curtailed in 1953, but would be briefly continued in 1955.

**TOP LEFT** From the front, it is clear that the 122mm D-49 gun with its massive mantlet collar and mantlet is offset from the centreline.

**TOP RIGHT** The 122mm D-49 gun mantlet was usually covered by a shroud in service.

**ABOVE LEFT** While the 122mm M-62T gun as used in the later T-10M was considered for the SU-122-54, the 122mm D-49 that was similar to the D-30 with the exception of the bore evacuator was mounted on production vehicles.

**ABOVE CENTRE** The left front of the Kubinka vehicle, showing the tow cable stowage and the headlight and marker light with their associated protected power cables.

**ABOVE RIGHT** The only other surviving SU-122-54 is located in Krasnodar in southern Russia. It has had most ancillary equipment removed over the years.

After the usual cycle of findings and corrections, the new assault gun was approved by Resolution No. 438-194 of the Council of Ministers on 15 March 1954 for production and service with the Soviet Army as the SU-122-54. While some early assessments indicated that 250 were built, data from Omsk plant records indicates that only 77 were made during a particularly short production run from 1954 to 1956.

The main armament ultimately installed in the SU-122-54 was the

**ABOVE LEFT** The SU-122-54 was unique among vehicles of its day, being fitted with a stereoscopic coincidence rangefinder for the gunner. The gun commander was seated at the left rear of the hull and provided with his own cupola.

**ABOVE RIGHT** The stereoscopic coincidence rangefinder was located in a purpose-designed armoured housing.

modified 122mm D-49, which had been approved for installation in the vehicle after final testing of the weapon against both the 122mm D-25T and 122mm M-62T guns, work on the latter having been revived in 1955 with a new breech and loading mechanism.

The modified 122mm D-49 was approved for installation in the vehicle and this weapon was installed in the production versions. The gun was essentially a 122mm D-25T but fitted with a fume extractor approximately one-third of the barrel length rearward from the muzzle.

The vehicle also featured heavy secondary armament, with one 14.5mm Vladimirov KPVT heavy machine gun mounted co-axially with the main gun and a second weapon mounted on a tourelle mounting for the loader on

The SU-122-54 had a well-designed casemate hull from a ballistic standpoint. Note the interlocked armour plates.

**ABOVE LEFT** The track guards on the SU-122-54 do not attach directly to the hull casemate. Note the mix of original and later 'starfish' road wheels.

**ABOVE RIGHT** The SU-122-54 engine deck was virtually identical to that used on the T-54 from which it was developed.

the left. The commander sat to the right of the gun with a cupola fitted with a TDK-09 stereoscopic rangefinder. The gunner was provided with a TSh2-24 sight that was fitted with reticules for both the D-49 and KPVT. He also had an S-71-24 panoramic sight that could be used with normal artillery measures for firing to a range of 13,400 metres; direct fire range was 4,000 metres with AP (armour-piercing) and 6,000 metres with HE-FRAG (high explosive fragmentation) rounds. The SU-122-54 carried 35 separate loading ammunition rounds and 1,000 rounds of 14.5mm.

Experiments were made in 1952 and again in 1955 to mount both the newer 122mm M-62T gun (as the Obiekt 620) and even the 130mm M-46 gun, which was developed as a paper design exercise, but these variants were ultimately dropped.

The SU-122-54 was based on the T-54 hull, but with the second and third road wheel station locations moved forward 250mm so the road wheels were closer together to better distribute the weight of the vehicle. For many years this confused Western experts, who considered that the SU-122-54 was actually based on the later T-62 chassis. Glacis armour protection was 100mm set at 51° from vertical. The casemate hull sides were 80mm set at 26° from vertical.

The SU-122-54 was mechanically otherwise identical to contemporary line T-54 tanks then in production (i.e. the T-54 Model 1951).

The 14.5mm KPVT anti-aircraft machine gun was mounted on the commander's cupola at the rear of the casemate fighting compartment.

**TOP LEFT** The SU-122-54 only had two external fuel tanks, both of which were conformal and located at the right rear of the casemate. In side profile, the excellent ballistic shape of the SU-122-54 is apparent.
**TOP RIGHT** When the SU-122-54 was removed from service, a small number (ten+) were converted to TOP parade recovery tractors. The gun opening and two of the roof hatches were plated over, and additional hatches fitted in the casemate rear wall. The vehicle was used for parade sentry duty as late as 1995.
**ABOVE LEFT** A view of the rear of the TOP vehicle casemate, showing the twin hatches for crew and equipment use. Note also the extra tow cables for the new recovery vehicle role.
**ABOVE RIGHT** Due to the timing of its public introduction, the TOP was initially thought to be a recovery variant of the T-62 MBT. This TOP vehicle, shown during the Victory Parade in Moscow on 9 May 1995, is fitted with IR headlights for the driver-mechanic and a standard T-54B cupola for the commander. The outline of the welded-in plate covering the gun aperture is just visible. Note also the raised driving position and consider the steering linkages!

The fighting compartment roof of the SU-122-54 with the stereoscopic coincidence rangefinder on the right and (the remains of) the KPVT AAMG mounting on the left.

The SU-122-54 was short-lived, as service deployment of heavy tanks, such as the T-10 series, and soon thereafter the arrival of 'PTUR' (anti-tank guided rockets) mounted on light vehicles made the role of the SU-122-54 redundant. A number of SU-122-54s were converted to the BMR (BMR-1) mine-clearing vehicle, in which role they were deployed in Afghanistan in the 1970s, modern conflicts in the Caucasus republics, mine-clearing operations in Lebanon and the civil war in modern Ukraine.

Some SU-122-54s were converted into MTP-3 (Машина Технической Помощи) – technical support and recovery vehicles – fitted with specialist recovery and repair equipment, while some others (approximately ten) were converted into TOP (Тягач Обеспечения Парадов) – parade recovery vehicles – provided with a set of tow cables only. In all cases the armament was removed and the gun aperture plated over.

Two prototypes of the Obiekt 610 'Buyvol' artillery mobile command post were built on converted SU-122-54 chassis in 1955 for trials, but they never entered service. A single SU-122-54 was converted into a BTS-600 (unofficially known as the BTS-5) recovery vehicle by the Lvov (now Lviv) Tank Repair Plant in Ukraine. The project was carried out in 1971 based on a design developed by the Kharkov Tank Repair Plant design bureau.

## ZSU-57-2 SELF-PROPELLED ANTI-AIRCRAFT GUN

At the end of World War II, anti-aircraft protection for Red Army armoured units was limited to local defence 'Dushka' (12.7mm DShK) weapons turret-mounted on tanks, and towed anti-aircraft artillery. In 1945–46 a small production series of tracked ZSU-37 self-propelled anti-aircraft guns

**UPPER** As the ZSU-57-2 could not use OPVT equipment, experiments were carried out to fit the PST flotation device to the vehicle. The complete PST floatation set is mounted on this ZSU-57-2 PST on land.

**LOWER** As with the heavier T-54, the PST pontoons greatly increased the dimensions of the vehicle when fitted.

**TOP LEFT** When swimming, the ZSU-57 PST did not have a great degree of freeboard, but was stable enough to fire.
**TOP RIGHT** For movement on land, the PST-fitted vehicle could fold up the outer pontoon sections, but the bow and stern ones still made the vehicle much longer than a standard ZSU-57-2.
**ABOVE LEFT** Due to the low freeboard, a trunk was fitted around the radiator grilles on the rear deck. Note that sufficient clearance has been left to allow turret traverse while waterborne.
**ABOVE CENTRE** The public debut of the ZSU-57-2 in Red Square, Moscow, on 7 November 1957. Organizations varied, but most ZSU-57-2s were organized into regiments of five or six batteries of four ZSU guns each.
**ABOVE RIGHT** A slightly later parade, with the ZSU-57-2s now given 'parade' markings, guards symbols and white striping.
**OPPOSITE** Another view during the same parade. For parade purposes, only four of the five turret crew are visible in this photo.

had been built, but mass production had not ensued. It was clear, however, that the post-war Soviet Army required an anti-aircraft vehicle that could engage faster and more powerful ground attack aircraft (*shturmoviki* to the Russians) and the emerging threat of helicopters. Single, dual and quadruple 14.5mm KPV machine gun mounts were introduced into Soviet Army service from 1949, but these were towed weapons. The Soviet Army required

**OPPOSITE TOP** The preserved ZSU-57-2 in the Kubinka collection. The vehicle is in good condition, having been in a particularly secure setting for decades.
**OPPOSITE CENTRE LEFT** The ZSU-57-2 resembles a T-54 but is made of much thinner armour. The turret is welded together from sheet steel pressings.
**OPPOSITE CENTRE RIGHT** The lightweight open turret allows for rapid traverse but limited protection for the crew. The turret floor is supported on steel support struts.
**OPPOSITE BOTTOM** Unlike the T-54, the headlights on the ZSU-57-2 are moved out onto the track guards.

a mobile anti-aircraft system vehicle capable of maintaining pace with Soviet armoured units on the march.

The Soviet Army received a new towed anti-aircraft weapon from 1950, the 57mm S-60, which would later prove efficient during the Korean War, and a mobile version was developed specifically for the protection of armoured units. In accordance with a resolution of the Council of Ministers dated 22 June 1948, Plant No. 174 in Omsk was tasked with creating a new self-propelled anti-aircraft gun based on the T-54 Model 1947 chassis. The project, designated Obiekt-500, was developed under the leadership of I. S. Bushnev.

Project designs and working drawings for the new gun, now designated ZSU-57-2 S-68, were approved in May 1949 and two prototypes were built in 1950. After testing, evaluation and modification, the ZSU-57-2 was accepted for service with the Soviet Army on 14 February 1955. Between 1957 and the end of production in 1960 Plant No. 174 built 2,023 ZSU-57-2 guns.

This vehicle underwent capital rebuilding at some point and now features the 'starfish' wheels of the later T-54s and T-55s. As the ZSU-57-2 is much lighter than the T-54, it only needs four road wheel pairs per side.

**TOP LEFT** While the ZSU-57-2 was designed to provide mobile anti-aircraft firepower to tactical forces, it was not expected to be in direct fire range, so the driver-mechanic was provided with a simple sheet steel flap that lifted to provide better vision.

**TOP RIGHT** The 57mm S-68 was capable of firing 240 rounds per minute (120 per barrel) and so a large bin was fitted at the turret rear to catch the expended shell casings. The rear opened for emptying the bin.

**ABOVE LEFT** The ZSU-57-2 could mount the 200-litre auxiliary fuel tanks, but as the rear plate was very thin it required extra bracing to prevent breaking or bending the mounts when installed. Note the pass-through within the braces for the unditching log.

**ABOVE RIGHT** The expended rounds were ejected via a slot in the rear of the turret into the catch bin.

The new ZSU-57-2 used a much lightened T-54 chassis with only four road wheels per side rather than five, an 18mm armour basis, and a bullet-resistant armoured open turret, within which was mounted the new S-68 twin 57mm anti-aircraft gun mounting. The driver-mechanic's position was unchanged from the T-54, with the remainder of the five-man crew dispersed within the new turret. The commander was on the right, the gunner on the left, with a loader on each side.

The vehicle carried 300 rounds of 57mm ammunition of which 248 were stored in four-round clips around the interior walls of the turret and the remaining 52 stowed below the turret floor. Each gun was capable of firing

**TOP LEFT** The 57mm S-68 was essentially two of the powerful S-60 guns mounted in parallel and configured into a single mounting. Even today the Russians are finding new uses for the calibre and its very effective rounds.

**TOP CENTRE** The ZSU-57-2 had a crew of six, of whom five were located in the turret (commander, gunner, aimer, and a loader for each barrel). 176 rounds in four-round clips were stowed around the inside of the turret, so the turret was quite cosy.

**TOP RIGHT** A preserved ZSU-57-2 at the Lubuskie Museum in Poland. This vehicle is missing many of its external fittings.

**ABOVE LEFT** The ZSU did not have any OPVT fittings as it could not submerge with its open turret. A tarpaulin was provided for strategic storage or when not in use. Lubuskie Museum, Poland

**ABOVE RIGHT** The independent 57mm guns are linked by a bolted mounting, ensuring accurate fire configuration. The guns are both fired by the gunner. Lubuskie Museum, Poland

100–120 rounds per minute, so the new self-propelled mount could fire 200–240 rounds per minute. The lightweight turret supported tracking speeds of 30° per second and the guns had a maximum angles of elevation of 85°.

The 28-metric tonne combat weight ZSU-57-2 carried 640 litres of fuel, which gave it a road range of approximately 420km. The ZSU-57-2 was otherwise mechanically identical to, and equipped as for, standard T-54 tanks then in series production (i.e. T-54 Model 1951).

Two later experimental variants of the ZSU-57-2 were built and tested. The Obiekt 510 was fitted with amphibious equipment for traversing open waterways. The Obiekt 520 was an upgrade to the basic ZSU-57-2, fitted with the 'Desna' electro-optical sighting system and the 'Berezina' gun mount. Tested under the project name 'Dnepr' from July 1958 to July 1959, the system was not ultimately adopted for service.

The ZSU-57-2 was originally deployed at divisional and then at regimental level, and a number were sold abroad to Soviet client states. While the ZSU-57-2 never saw combat service with the Soviet Army, it saw widespread use in foreign wars, including during the Vietnam War and the 1967 'Six Day War' in the Middle East. The ZSU-57-2 remains in service with smaller armies today.

## ARMOURED ENGINEER VEHICLES

### MTU-12 (MTU-1) TANK BRIDGE-LAYER

The European part of the Soviet Union is traversed by an inordinate number of rivers, lakes and small streams, and the Red Army as early as the 1930s introduced a doctrine of developing the means to cross such obstacles, which included amphibious tanks and armoured cars, and specialized bridge-layer tanks. In the 1930s the Red Army had experimented with tank-launched assault bridges to ensure that armoured units could maintain offensive capability by crossing small streams, damaged bridges or shell craters in roads. Experimental versions were built using the T-26 light tank, the BT series fast tanks, and finally one version based on a modified T-28 medium

Another subject for An-22 air transport trials was the MTU-12 bridge-layer. This training vehicle is shown with a tarpaulin over the bridge.

**TOP LEFT** A side view of the MTU-12 with a measuring stick propped up next to it for scale.
**TOP RIGHT** A front view of the same MTU-12 bridge-layer.
**ABOVE LEFT** The MTU-12 inside the mock-up An-22 cargo bay. Due to the length of the bridge only one could be carried, a size rather than weight restriction.
**ABOVE RIGHT** A front view of the MTU-12 inside the An-22 'fuselage'. A tight fit.

tank chassis. But while the concept met with reasonable success, none of these designs were produced in quantity and the idea was shelved during World War II.

In the early 1950s the idea was revived at Plant No. 183 (UVZ) under the designation K-67. Two prototypes were built at the plant in early 1953 and underwent range testing in April and May of that year. After some further development at Plant No. 75 in Kharkov, they were sent for service testing by engineer troops. The vehicle was approved for service and was series produced at Plant No. 75 from 1955 to 1960, at which point the plant switched over to the use of the T-55 tank chassis.

The concept was to use a 12.26-metre-long single section brigade capable of supporting the crossing of medium and heavy tanks, with a maximum 50-metric tonne combat weight (i.e. including the IS-3 and new

OPPOSITE TOP LEFT The MTU-12 was the first dedicated Soviet armoured bridge-layer to enter production and service. Using a T-54 hull, the vehicle transported a fixed 12-metre treadway bridge.
OPPOSITE TOP RIGHT The 12-metre bridge had a significant overhang in front and behind the hull, so the driver-mechanic required skill manoeuvring in built-up areas.
OPPOSITE The launcher mechanism resembles that tested on the T-28-based MT-28 bridge-layer in the 1930s. The system used a truck-type axle to transfer drive from the engine and massive chains to move the bridge forward on its launcher cradle.
ABOVE LEFT The MTU-12 hull was fitted with most of the standard T-54 ancillaries, including a pair of MDK smoke canisters and an unditching log.
ABOVE RIGHT A very sturdy bracket was mounted at the rear of the MTU-12 to support the bridge when travelling. (All photographs: Artillery, Engineer & Communications Museum, St Petersburg)

T-10 heavy tanks). The ammunition stowage was removed from the hull and a new position with a hatch installed for the vehicle commander to the right of the driver-mechanic. A position was provided for a machine gunner in the centre of the hull, equipped with a 12.7mm DShKM machine gun on a tourelle ring mount located in the centre of the bridge in travel mode. The weapon could also be moved to a pintle mount on the vehicle hull.

Launching the bridge was accomplished by approaching the obstacle until it was felt that the front edge of the bridge would be firmly supported on its opposite side. The bridge was cranked out from the tank by cables and a winch on a special support frame that the tank used to both launch and recover the bridge. The bridge took 2–3 minutes to launch and 5–8 minutes to recover.

As with any tank-mounted bridging system, the longer the bridge the better, with the limitation being bridge dimensions, bridge and overall system weight, and the launch and recovery mechanism. In 1962, a 16-metre aluminium construction bridge was designed for the MTU-12. However, the more practical 20-metre MTU-20 bridge mounted on the T-55 chassis was by then in production, so further work was terminated.

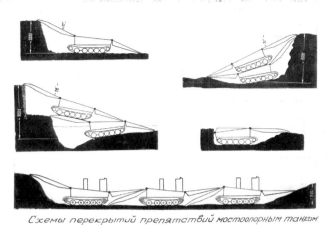

Схемы перекрытий препятствий мостоопорным танком

**ABOVE LEFT** Inspired by the Churchill and Sherman Ark tanks used by the British, Soviet designers developed a local variant as the MOT.
**ABOVE RIGHT** The prototype MOT under test as a bridge-layer. Note the three snorkels for air intake and exhaust while the hull is submerged.

## MOT BRIDGE-LAYER

The British experimented with the use of tanks as bridging vehicles in World War II, with Churchill tank chassis fitted with folding ramps being used for crossing anti-tank ditches, seawalls, and other obstacles that would most likely stop tank movement or place the tank in immediate danger of destruction from enemy anti-tank means. These bridge-layer vehicles were used in combat by the 79th Armoured Division and noted some successes.

After the war the Soviet Army also turned its attention in this direction. In 1948 a joint project between Plant No. 75 and GBTU resulted in a model and plans for such a vehicle being produced during that year. A prototype was built at Plant No. 75 in 1949 based on a T-54 hull and components.

The MOT (MostoOpornyy Tank) was designed to serve as a bridge for vehicles of up to 75 metric tonnes to negotiate obstacles of up to 15.5 metres wide or 5.5 metres in height. The vehicle was fitted with front and rear 3.6-metre-wide folding ramps, featured stiffened sides and platforms, and had a 1.3-metre-wide centre gap. For wider obstacles, two or more MOT vehicles could be 'daisy chained' together.

The MOT bridging bridge-layer tank could ford up to 1.3 metres of water without preparation, but due to its requirement to be used in rivers it was fitted with an OPVT underwater driving system to bring that wading depth up to 3.8 metres. The vehicle had a crew of three and no armament.

Testing of the MOT vehicle showed it to be quite limited in its abilities and it was therefore cancelled in favour of more advanced bridge-launcher vehicles.

# MINE- AND OBSTACLE-CLEARING VEHICLES

## PT-54 MINE TRAWL

The wartime Red Army referred to mine-roller systems as 'tralshiki' or mine trawls, and this term remains in use today. During World War II the Red Army used the PT-3 mine trawl, which consisted of a set of heavy solid cast steel wheels mounted on a forward projecting beam, to clear paths through mine fields. It was logical that this would continue with the post-war T-54 tank series, and work on the theme was undertaken at Plant No. 75 from 1948, with two prototype systems based on the PT-3 built in October of that year. After testing and further development, two more prototypes were built in May 1949, which underwent plant trials, followed by eight more, which were issued to the Soviet Army for service testing in June 1949. Per a resolution of the Council of Ministers dated 14 July 1950, the PT-54 mine trawl was accepted for service with the Soviet Army.

**TOP** The Red Army had used what were designated 'mine trawls' – rollers used to clear anti-tank and anti-personnel mines – during World War II, such as the PT-3 on the T-34 tanks. An updated version was trialled on the T-54, starting with the Model 1947.

**LEFT** The system was simple: six heavy cast rollers were fitted to a frame attached to the front of the tank and capable of moving in a vertical axis. When the rollers hit a mine, the assembly would be lifted by the explosion but not usually terminally damaged.

The rollers left a central gap, but fully covered the track width of the mine roller tank. A prototype with a third roller assembly mounted behind the tank was tested as Obiekt 413, but did not progress beyond trials stage.

For transport purposes the PT-54 was carried in two ZiL-151 6x6 trucks. The PT-54 could be fitted to the T-54 lower glacis manually, but was usually fitted using a truck-mounted crane. The trawl consisted of two sections with six rollers on each, with each set of rollers clearing a strip 1.3 metres wide. Clearing speed was 8–12km/h, and it was determined that each unit could take the detonations of 20 TM-46 class anti-tank mines before needing replacement. When fitted with the mine trawls, the tank was, however, limited in its manoeuvrability; maximum speed with the trawl fitted was only 30km/h. The tanks concerned also required special fittings to mount the mine trawl.

## COMBINATION MINE TRAWL (OBIEKT 413)

Mine trawls such as the PT-54 had one fundamental flaw – they left a gap between their roller sets that could possibly lead to casualties for following infantry. The 'P. M. Mugalev' Military Engineering Academy thereby, in 1951, proposed a new version for medium tanks. The academy, which specialized in mine clearance systems, proposed a system using three sections of mine roller wheels similar to the PT-3 and PT-54 designs. Two sections were mounted in front of the tank, as with the PT-3 and PT-54, and one was towed behind the tank to cover the central gap left by the forward pair. The complete system weighed 13.3 metric tonnes.

**ABOVE** The T-54 was rebuilt, mainly from Model 1947 tanks, into a dedicated mine-clearing vehicle known as the BMR-2. It could mount a number of alternative mine ploughs or mine trawls, and this vehicle has a trawl frame mounted.

**LEFT** Here is a Ukrainian-built BMR-2 fitted with one of several later track-width mine ploughs.

**BELOW** A frontal view of the same BMR-2 vehicle.

**ABOVE** Another view of a BMR-2 , this time on the move with the frame in place and elevated for transit.
**BELOW** A BMR-2 fitted with rollers lowered into the operating position.

In the second half of 1952, Plant No. 75 re-designed the trawl with seven wheels in each section, with the trawl weight increased to 13.8 metric tonnes. This was 5 metric tonnes more than the PT-54 trawl, and required a third all-terrain cargo truck to transport it when not in use. The system was more expensive, and was also deemed to seriously limit the host tank's mobility, and was therefore dropped.

## PT-55 MINE TRAWL

The PT-55 mine trawl, while designed for use on the later T-55 tank as a further development of the PT-54, was interchangeable with the earlier PT-54 and used on T-54 tanks. Developed in 1959, the PT-55 weighed 6.7 to 7 metric tonnes, but cleared a strip only 0.83 metres wide in front of the tracks. The new system could also only withstand the equivalent of ten TM-46 anti-tank mine blasts, while the discs did not penetrate as deeply into the ground ahead of the tank.

Manoeuvrability of the T-54/T-55 with the PT-55 mine trawl fitted was poor – turning the tank in a mine field with the trawl deployed required a turn radius of 85 metres, which was reduced to 9 metres with the system lifted and neutral steer used to turn the tank.

The PT-55 took 10–15 minutes to install with a crane, and dismounting took 3–5 minutes. The major advantage of the newer system was that the speed of movement in minefields was faster with the PT-55, and clearing speeds of 15–20km/h were noted. The system required three trucks to transport it, including the marker assembly that was fitted at the rear of the hull to show the path cleared by the tank.

Most of the later mine trawl developments, such as the KMT-4 and KMT-5, could also be mounted on older T-54 tanks fitted to use mine trawl equipment.

The BTU-54 was designed early in the life of the T-54 tank series and is seen here on test, fitted to a T-54 Model 1947. The shoe in the front is used as a depth gauge to keep the plough from entrenching too deeply and causing the tank to stall.

**ABOVE** From the front the width of the plough mouldboard is seen to be wider than the tank. This blade was fixed and could not be reconfigured to a straight-edge plough as in some later designs.
**BELOW** A cross-section from a Soviet manual, showing how the BTU-54 mounted to the upper and lower glacis of the tank.

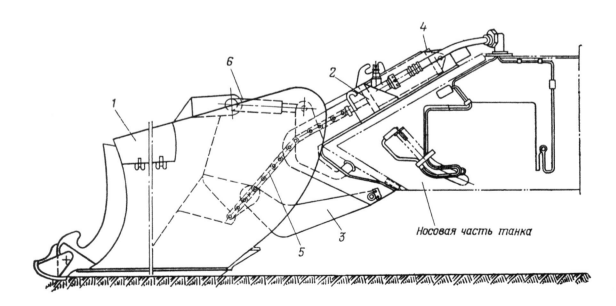

Носовая часть танка

## BTU (BTU-54) STANDARDIZED TANK BULLDOZER

As with the United States and Great Britain, which had both fitted bulldozer blades to standard tanks for use in combat situations for obstacle clearing, road smoothing, filling in craters and bunkers under fire, and digging positions for use by tanks and self-propelled guns for defensive fire, the Soviet Army also decided it needed a bulldozer fitting for its medium tanks.

A BTU (BTU-54) blade system was developed specifically for the T-54, and was designed for fitment to the bow of line tanks without any major re-design required of the tank. This bulldozer had a mouldboard with a width of 3.4 metres and a depth of 1.1 metres, with a built-in folding depth control shoe located in the centre of the blade. The tank could plough to a depth of 0.2 metres on each pass with the shoe in place or 0.45 metres with it folded. The tank in this situation could move 100–230 cubic metres of earth per hour. This would permit one tank to dig three to five tank defensive positions per hour.

Fitting the bulldozer assembly to the tank took 1.5–2 hours, but removing it only required 30–40 minutes. Dropping the blade from travel to working position took five seconds. The driver-mechanic had the blade controls added to his control levers inside the tank. The blade was raised and lowered by chains attached to hydraulic cylinders. The blade weighed 2.3 metric tonnes, and when installed the blade limited maximum speed to 16–18km/h in travel mode or 3–6km/h in working mode.

The BTU-54 was replaced by the BTU-55 in 1963, but both could be fitted to a T-54 tank equipped with the required bolt mounts under the bow of the tank.

## STU-2 SNOW PLOUGH

One of the lesser-known functions for T-54 tanks was their use as snow plough vehicles when required, for which purpose a universal snow plough was designed for the tank. This was created in 1954 and tested at the NIIBT range in Kubinka.

The plough was based on the old STU-38 plough but now fitted with electric motors for raising and lowering the blade. The plough was a twin blade arrangement which could clear a width of 3.3 metres on each pass; two passes would clear a strip 4.7 metres wide and three passes 6.2 metres. Operational speed was 5–8km/h, but the tank could move at 15–20km/h with the blade raised. Fitting the plough to the tank required help from a mobile repair base for fitting the mounts to the lower hull and rigging the frame to the upper glacis. The plough weighed 2,450kg and required 25–35 minutes to fit once the mounts were installed, and 15–20 minutes to remove.

An improved model, the STU-2M, was introduced in 1961.

**TOP LEFT** A frontal view of a T-54B fitted with the PST-54 pontoon set. The PST-54 was obviously awkward to manoeuvre on land.
**TOP RIGHT** The Soviets tested the PST-54 in a 'sea state' of 1 to 5 *ballov* (points) as a measure of seaworthiness. Here one of the tanks is swimming in a '2-*balla*' (2-point) sea state at maximum speed (7–10km/h).
**ABOVE** To allow the T-54 to cross water obstacles, whether rivers or open water, a set of pontoons designated PST-54 was developed for the tank. Here a prototype set fitted to a Model 1949 tank is undergoing integrity trials.
**RIGHT** A T-54 PST with its bulky pontoons exiting the water over a steep sand bank.

## ST-3 SNOW PLOUGH

In 1948 an attempt was made to design a universal snow plough that would fit on the hulls of the T-34, T-44 and T-54. But while the plough was manufactured and tested, it was found there was no way of providing a single set of fitments compatible with all three tanks, and as a result the ST-3 was dropped.

## AMPHIBIOUS CROSSING EQUIPMENT

### PST-54 SWIMMING EQUIPMENT

During World War II, Allied and Axis forces both worked on amphibious equipment that would allow tanks to float so that they could swim ashore or cross rivers in combat situations. But only the Japanese developed these

**TOP LEFT** Here two PST-equipped tanks are moving along a road with their outer pontoons folded in.
**TOP RIGHT** This T-54B is about to be fitted with its side pontoons, which are lying on the ground next to it.
**ABOVE** With the turret reversed and a portable jib crane rigged on the turret rear, the pontoons are being attached to the hull front.
**ABOVE CENTRE** Fitting the frontal pontoon and wave breaker to the hull mounts.
**ABOVE RIGHT** The moment of jettisoning the pontoons on dry land. The OPVT system offered much less difficult and awkward means for relatively short distance water crossing with tanks, and the PST-54 system, primarily designed for open water travel, was ultimately dropped.

tanks as 'standard' designs, and information on their use swimming under combat conditions is at best somewhat sketchy.

Nevertheless, the Russians decided they needed such equipment for the

On being declared obsolete, the SU-122-54 was modified as the MTP-3 tank repair and recovery vehicle, fitted with specialist recovery and repair equipment. A single SU-122-54 was also converted into a BTS-600 (unofficially known as BTS-5) in 1971 at the Lvov (now Lviv) Tank Repair Plant.

Soviet Army, and so Plant No. 174 and the 'Novoshinskiy' Ship Building Plant No. 342 combined their efforts between 1944 and 1957 to produce such equipment. But while prototypes were made and tested it was not until September 1957 that the idea came to fruition, when a group of tanks used the equipment to successfully swim in open water on Lake Ehzel' (the water by what is today Saaremaa Island in the Baltic Sea – offshore modern Latvia).

This equipment, dubbed the PST-54 ('Tank Swimming Means – 54'), as it was designed for use with the T-54 tank, saw 73 sets made to fit to T-54B tanks built specifically for the purpose by Plant No. 75 in Kharkov.

The system consisted of four pontoons attached to the tank at the sides and front and rear of the hull using transverse trusses, brackets on the front, and a rear pedestal mount. The system weighed 9.3 metric tonnes, and was considered seaworthy enough to withstand a stage four (4-*balla* in Russian) sea state. Propulsion came from two propellers powered via a power-take-off mechanism. The tank could thus swim at speeds of up to 10km/h and even fire its guns at sea states of stage 1.5 or less (1.5-*balla*). But it required four dedicated cargo trucks to carry the system when not mounted. Installation required 35 minutes with a prepared vehicle. Fittings were in place for the crew to drop the pontoons on landing nearly instantaneously.

However, with the drawback that it required careful engineering preparation of the beaches or banks of a river for use, and the fact that the newer OPVT equipment had been created, there were no further actions in this area (mobile ferries were then designed to carry tanks across wider and deeper obstacles).

## PST-U SWIMMING EQUIPMENT

The PST-U was a derivative of the PST-54 system, designed by Omsk and Plant No. 342 between 1958 and 1959 and specifically designed to permit the ZSU-57-2 to swim in the same manner as the so-modified T-54B tanks, but the system could also be fitted to the T-54 or T-55 tank. Slightly larger and heavier than the PST-54, the PST-U used its own diesel engines for power and could swim at up to 12.4km/h. It was assessed that a tank or ZSU could swim for a distance of up to 100km with the system fitted.

Due to its larger overall dimensions, the PST-U required two ZiL-157 trucks with semi-trailers for transport purposes.

During trials, it was noted that the ZSU-57-2 could fire its guns while waterborne as long as the sea state was not more than stage 2 (2-*balla*), which allowed for the effective defence of amphibious landing operations.

# REPAIR AND ARMOURED RECOVERY VEHICLES

## BTS-2 MEDIUM TANK TRACTOR

During World War II the Red Army had taken worn-out or obsolete models of tanks and converted them into recovery tractors and light repair vehicles for the battlefield recovery of damaged tanks of the same or lighter class for repair and rebuild. While the early vehicles were based on T-34, KV and occasionally IS chassis, which continued to be used in the immediate post-war era, a new model based on the T-54 chassis was needed for the post-war Soviet Army of the 1950s.

The new T-54 based armoured recovery vehicle (ARV) design was tasked to N. A. Shomin at UVZ and was specifically noted to be a high-speed tractor capable of recovering medium and heavy tanks of up to 75 metric tonnes from the battlefield, and for towing inoperable tanks and self-propelled guns on roads. The prototype, designated Obiekt 9, was developed between 1947 and 1951, followed by manufacturing plant testing. Three reworked prototypes were then

sent to the NIIBT test range at Kubinka for testing from January to May 1952. There followed several more changes and improvements to the winch design in 1953 and 1954, after which the vehicle was recommended for production.

Among other features of the prototypes, one was a tourelle ring and mount for a 12.7mm DShK machine gun provided for use by the radio operator. The mounting was heavy and awkward to use, however, with low accuracy of fire, and as a result it was dropped from production vehicles.

The new ARV vehicle was accepted for service as the BTS-2 by a resolution of the Council of Ministers dated 21 February 1955, and an establishment lot of ten vehicles was built in 1956. Series production was authorized the following year. An interesting nuance is that the ten establishment lot vehicles were armed with a 7.62mm AK assault rifle fitted with a curved barrel for firing from within a vehicle – it was discontinued during series production.

The new BTS-2 had a crew of three, consisting of a driver-mechanic/commander, radio operator, and a specialist/rigger, all of whom sat in the control compartment. For local defence they were provided with personal weapons and grenades. The centre portion of the upper hull was occupied by a cargo platform with a capacity of 4 metric tonnes for equipment, fuel and lubricants, spare engine and transmission components, and other items. A folding manual crane with post and two braces was provided, as well as a large spade anchor at the rear of the hull. Also provided was a winch of 25 metric tonnes maximum pull, with a 200-metre cable plus sheaves and pulleys for towing or recovering damaged vehicles. The tractive effort could be increased to 50 or 75 metric tonnes by doubling or tripling the pulley sheaves and cable rigging. For simple towing the

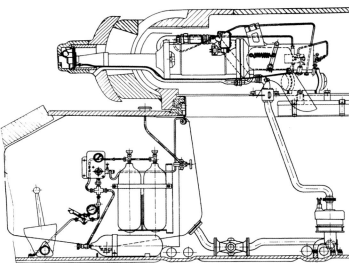

vehicle had two 4.1-metre tow cables with a tensile force of 15 metric tonnes each.

The BTS-2 weighed 32 metric tonnes and most of its other equipment was identical to that of the later production T-54 tanks. The BTS-2 was followed by the BTS-4, which was a complete rebuild of obsolete T-44 tanks as recovery tractors.

An earlier development, the BTS-1, did not have a winch or other essential elements needed for successful recovery and apparently was only produced in small numbers for trials purposes.

# FLAMETHROWER TANKS

## TO-54 FLAMETHROWER TANK

Experience from World War II showed that the use of flamethrower tanks based on line tanks worked better than dedicated vehicles in action, so as the T-54 series was being developed it was decided to ensure there was a flamethrower variant of that tank for use by chemical troops (who handled all flame weapons in the Soviet Army and even today in the Russian Army).

In 1948 Plant No. 112 in Gorky (today Nizhny Novgorod) began working on adapting the wartime ATO-42 tank flamethrower for installation on the new T-54 tank. But during trials the configuration was found to be unreliable and work was terminated.

The Obiekt 481 prototype on test, showing the similarity to a standard T-54 Model 1951 tank when viewed from a distance. This tank does not feature the front 95-litre fuel tank.

**TOP LEFT** The Obiekt 483 had to do away with the co-axial machine gun and special sights were provided for ranging the target.
**TOP RIGHT** The central projector was surrounded by venturis to help keep it cool when firing and ensure the flame stream received sufficient oxygen for good combustion.
**ABOVE LEFT** The commander was provided with a special sight to assist in locating and ranging targets.
**ABOVE RIGHT** Changes at the rear of the turret included a new ventilator and a rear hatch for both refuelling the internal tanks, filling the compressed air tanks, and replacing/servicing the flame projector.

Further work was carried out by SKB-1 in Kharkov under F. A. Mostovoy per a resolution of the Council of Ministers dated 10 July 1948. This was done in conjunction with work undertaken by NII-6 in Moscow, which set up Specialized Flamethrower Laboratory No. 12 to work on this task. Requirements were for a range of 200–300 metres, with a burst of 20 litres of flame fuel.

Work was passed over to SKB-1 chief M. S. Ozersky. The new system, dubbed ATO-49, was built as a prototype in March 1949, but testing showed it to have some serious defects and so it went back for re-design.

Per a resolution of the Council of Ministers dated 17 December 1949, Plant No. 75 built two new models during the first half of 1950. During testing in 1951 these new prototypes also failed to meet expectations. Seeing some technical problems with the original design remit, a new resolution of the Council of Ministers dated 19 October 1951 reduced the range expectations from 200–300 metres to only 180 metres, which would be achieved in windless conditions and with the flamethrower elevated to only 8°. Two prototype T-54 tanks fitted with the new system underwent testing in January 1952. Range was now dropped by official requirements to only 160–170 metres.

These tanks received the plant designation Obiekt 481, but even after modification they could not achieve even the lower range when tested in August 1952. After more attempts to correct the ATO-49, a new design, the UATO, was put forth in 1953; it proved too complex and was dropped.

Finally, after more reworking, the modified ATO-49, now dubbed the ATO-1, was accepted for service on 14 May 1954 by the Council of Ministers, and the tank was dubbed the TO-54.

The TO-54 was basically a production T-54 tank but with its co-axial machine gun replaced by the ATO-1 flame gun. It carried 460–470 litres of flame mixture internally in place of the 20 100mm rounds normally racked on the right side of the fighting compartment. Fitted with two 10-litre compressed air tanks fed from a larger compressor, the flamethrower could reach a range of 160 metres under ideal conditions, with 20 litres per burst and could fire up to 20 bursts a minute.

An improved model, designated ATO-200 as it could achieve the 200-metre range sought by the Soviet Army, was fitted to a T-54B tank in 1957 and given the designator Obiekt 482. This was later transferred to T-55 tanks when that tank entered production late in 1958. A total of 940 TO-54, TO-54B and TO-55 tanks were built fitted with the flamethrower system.

Later, a dedicated flamethrower version of the T-54, called Obiekt 483, was developed with the flame gun in place of the 100mm main gun. It was designed to carry 1,500 litres of flame mixture, but it did not succeed and only a single prototype was built.

# OTHER T-54 BASED PROJECTS

## OBIEKT 137G2M MEDIUM TANK

This prototype was envisaged as a modernized version of the T-54B tank. Offered as an initiative project to celebrate the 40th anniversary of the Great October Revolution in 1957, it was a vastly improved and simplified version of the T-54B, with many modifications and improvements added since the T-54 originally entered service. The tank was accepted for service on 24 May 1958 – but as the T-55 Medium Tank.

## OBIEKT 139

While the T-55 became the eventual successor to the T-54, there were other attempts made to upgrade it during the 1950s. As previously noted, Morozov had switched his design efforts to the Obiekt 430 and later Obiekt 432 projects that produced the T-64, but UVZ in Nizhny Tagil tried to remain true to the view of Leonid Kartsev to focus on evolution rather than revolution in producing new tank designs.

Per a resolution of the Council of Ministers dated 29 March 1952, Plant No. 183 tasked A. V. Kolesnikov to work with TsKB-393 and TsNII-173 to develop a two-axis stabilized gun sight for the T-54 tank. After scientific research work on the project, a later resolution dated 24 February 1955 authorized prototype design work to proceed. The new vehicle, designated Obiekt 139, was originally projected to enter service as the T-55 'Molniya' tank.

Manufacturing plant testing of the prototypes began in March 1956, but the sight suffered a number of serious defects. The system was removed from the prototypes for re-design after seven months of testing, and it was not until February 1959 that the tank returned to the test programme. During firing trials, one prototype fired 771 rounds and the second 591 rounds.

The tank used the new high-power 100mm D-54TS gun with two-axis stabilization and the T2SA 'Udar' prototype sight developed by Plant No. 393 in Krasnogorsk in the suburbs of Moscow. This gun had a muzzle velocity of 1,015m/s with AP ammunition, but the remaining components of the tank were identical to those of line T-54 tanks, with the exception of the side armour being reduced to 70mm due to the increased weight of the gun and stabilizer equipment.

While the tank design finally passed all testing, new tanks were by that time under development, and as a result the project was cancelled on 29 June 1962.

## OBIEKT 140 MEDIUM TANK

Of all of the Soviet tank prototypes that never saw production, it is arguable that the Obiekt 140 was the most influential of them all. The suspension developed for the Obiekt 140 was later used on the Obiekt 167 prototype and subsequently the Obiekt 172M, which became the T-72.

Based on a 1953 requirement to design the follow-on tank to the T-54, Morozov went to work on his own design, Obiekt 430, later to become the T-64. Kartsev meantime worked with the UVZ design bureau to develop its own new tank design, Obiekt 140. After undergoing assessment by the Scientific Technical Committee of the Main Armoured Tank Command

(NTK GBTU) in July 1954, the UVZ design bureau was authorized to develop the tank to prototype stage per a Council of Ministers resolution dated 6 May 1955.

Due to the laborious process of approval and stage evaluation, the first prototype did not emerge until May 1957. The prototype suffered from transmission problems and was prone to shed its rubber wheel rims due to the new suspension, and so required further rework.

The tank essentially used the hull of a T-54 with a large number of changes. First and foremost was a new suspension utilizing six smaller diameter road wheels and three return rollers, with substantial shock absorbers on road wheel stations 1 and 6. The tank was fitted with a turret based on the design of the T-54 but with a new turret race of 2,230mm, mounting a 100mm D-54TS gun with multi-baffle muzzle brake. The tank retained the now standard T-54 turret co-axial machine gun but upgraded the anti-aircraft machine gun to a 14.5mm KPVT. The Obiekt 140 also used the T2SA 'Udar' sight originally trialled on the Obiekt 139 prototype.

The glacis armour remained 100mm, but side armour varied from 57mm directly behind the wheels to 80mm above them. Turret protection was increased to 240mm at the front and 220mm on the sides. Obiekt 140 was provided with an ejection hatch in the turret rear for removing fired shell casings, the first Soviet tank to be provided with this feature. The tank carried 50 rounds for the main armament, 3,000 rounds of 7.62mm and 500 rounds of 14.5mm.

The Obiekt 140 prototype was fitted with a new TD-12 water-cooled diesel engine from Plant No. 77, replacing the older V-54 engine. The new engine produced 580hp, and instead of a single exhaust on the left side used one port under a grille on each side of the radiator air intake on the engine deck. Internal fuel capacity under armour was 825 litres, with an additional 275 litres mounted in tanks on the track guards.

The tank was relatively successful during trials and passed its final evaluation testing. However, it did not enter production, and for a number of reasons. One of them was that Kartsev believed and formally stated that the Obiekt 140 represented already obsolete technology and was not a step forward to improve the tank arm of the Soviet Army – nor was the competing Obiekt 430 in his opinion any better. This statement earned him the enmity of many senior tank officers and was considered one of many reasons his later Obiekt 167 was rejected out of hand, the T-62 was only accepted as a 'tank destroyer' and the initial T-72 versions were looked at as secondary compared with the more advanced but less reliable T-64s.

### OBIEKT 141 MEDIUM TANK

Obiekt 141 was developed in accordance with a resolution of the Council of Ministers dated 12 September 1952. The tank prototype was developed as a joint effort by Plant No. 9, Plant No. 183 and TsNII-173, mounting the new 100mm D-54T gun in a standard T-54 tank. This version of the D-54T was later also used in trials of the 'Raduga' stabilizer, but this effort was later replaced by the more advanced D-54TS gun with two-axis stabilizer. With the exception of the new D-54T armament, modified ammunition racks for the longer ammunition rounds and minor changes to the forward part of the turret, the tank was otherwise a standard T-54 Model 1951.

Obiekt-141 was not accepted for service for a number of reasons, the main one being the difficulty encountered by the loader in manipulating the longer rounds within the T-54 turret. The prototype was, however, later used as a test 'mule' for the bored-out 115mm smoothbore gun based on the D-54TS that became the U-5TS gun mounted on the T-62 tank. The tank was also used for testing the 'Zhelud' partial combustible case ammunition later adopted by the Soviet Army.

### OBIEKT 142 MEDIUM TANK

The Obiekt 142 tank was an attempt to mount the 100mm D-54 gun in a T-54B together with the new 'V'Yuga' gun stabilizer system. The tank was identical to a standard T-54B other than the new gun and fitments, but suffered the same problems as the Obiekt 141 with handling the longer rounds within the turret.

### OBIEKT 441 MEDIUM TANK

In the 1950s, Soviet military doctrine encompassed the newly emerging presence and probable use of tactical nuclear weapons on the battlefield. Soviet tank designers accordingly expended considerable design effort on developments to protect tanks from both shock wave and radiological effects. Plant No. 75 conducted work on this problem in accordance with GBTU requirements in 1956. The goal was to ensure that the focus tank could

An attempt was made to mount the powerful new 100mm D-54T rifled tank gun into a T-54 turret. The mounting proved capable to absorb the recoil, but the rounds were too long to easily handle in the turret and the idea was scrapped in favour of a totally new tank, Obiekt 165.

survive the blast and radiation from a small nuclear weapon (a 280mm artillery projectile was the given model) at a range of 300 metres from ground zero.

In March 1957 a prototype Obiekt 441 tank fitted with ZOMP (*Zashchita ot Oruzhiya Massovogo Porazheniya* – protection from weapons of mass destruction) underwent plant and Soviet Army operational testing. The system, now designated PAZ, was approved, with documentation sent to Plant No. 183 for application to tanks then in production. The PAZ system was installed on T-55 and T-55A tanks.

Basically, when switched on the PAZ system generated a slight overpressure within the tank, which prevented radioactive dust entering the fighting compartment. It was automatically triggered by a nuclear detonation near the vehicle, activating the system for crew protection and also closing the louvres over the engine compartment to prevent contamination entering there. Later – in the T-55A – the tanks were fitted with radiation protective liners within the tank.

## OBIEKT 442 MEDIUM TANK

Until the mid-1950s, Soviet tanks had generated smoke screens by means of two MDK or BDSh-5 smoke canisters, which were mounted on the rear of the tank. The decision to use the rear of the hull to carry additional fuel in from that time forward necessitated another solution. This was developed by Plant No. 75 as the thermal smoke generating system (TDA), which simply injected fuel directly into the exhaust, producing thick white clouds of smoke nearly instantaneously.

Per an agreement with GBTU dated 30 April 1955, Plant No. 75 worked on the design and in August 1957 produced a prototype. Testing showed the clouds of smoke produced were as thick as those from BDSh-5 canisters, but were far simpler and more durable (with weather being a consideration), with it also being possible to control the duration of the screen produced.

**BELOW LEFT** The helicopter gas turbine engine tank had a large compartment on the engine deck for monitoring of its operation and a venturi type exhaust. While the installation worked adequately, it was considered unviable. Later tests were conducted with the Obiekt 167T tank and a totally new engine arrangement.

**BELOW** A mania swept Soviet tank designers in the early 1960s to fit gas turbine engines to tanks. A T-54 chassis was used as a test-bed with a helicopter gas turbine engine installation. It fitted neatly into the engine bay, as seen here, and was provided with a two-speed automatic transmission for testing.

The TDA system was approved for manufacture, and in October 1957 Plant No. 183 began to fit it to the T-54B tank. After testing, it was initially applied to the T-54A, T-54B and then forthcoming T-55 tanks, but was later applied as standard on all Soviet tanks.

## OBIEKT 486 MEDIUM TANK

As with many other systems which entered production, OPVT underwater driving equipment was also tested on a specially assigned prototype vehicle. Based on a decision by the MTrM and GBTU dated 18 February 1955, Plant No. 75 produced three prototype tanks fitted with the OPVT-54 system in the third quarter of 1956. The tanks used for trials purposes were 1952 production models, which underwent operational unit testing in September and October of that year. After promising results, a decision was made on 9 January 1957 to place the system in production and install it on the T-54B tank. A total of 225 sets were made in the first year.

Eventually, several different versions were made: the OPVT-54 for T-54 Model 1951 tanks; OPVT-54A for T-54A tanks; OPVT-54B for T-54B tanks; and OPVT-54D for T-54 Model 1949 tanks. Each set came with specific fittings for that class of tank.

The equipment added 150kg to the combat weight of the tank. The system was provided with a two-section intake tube extending to a height of just over 5 metres from the ground to its intake opening, which was attached to the commander's hatch via a special fitting. This tube provided air induction for the crew and for the engine. Water sealing consisted of rubber and rubberized covers for the gun mantlet, the gunner's telescopic sight, co-axial machine gun, turret air ventilator, the engine air intake/radiator air intake on the engine deck, and rubber plugs for the openings in the lower hull. A one-way 'flapper' valve was fitted to the exhaust port on the left side of the tank, with a permanently mounted flange attached for that purpose. Two metal covers with sealing gaskets flipped over to cover the radiator air exhaust and the oil and transmission cooler air exhaust at the rear of the engine deck. An inflatable rubber seal was provided to seal the turret race from water. When stored, most of the equipment went into ZIP boxes on the track guards, while the two-section intake tube was nested and stored on two racks on the engine deck. Later, a four-section tube was introduced that nested and was stored on two brackets attached to the side of the turret.

Starting in April 1958, all T-54B tanks were produced with OPVT equipment as standard issue, with the new T-55 similarly equipped. Folding sealed metal covers for the engine radiator air intakes were later introduced and retroactively fitted to the T-54 series.

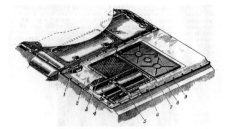

**ABOVE LEFT** The original rubberized canvas cover for the engine deck with the hatch for use while waiting to cross. The cover was bolted down to a special frame mounted over the engine deck.
**ABOVE RIGHT** The cover in place with the hatch open, which allowed air to circulate through the radiator and was then closed just before crossing. Water crossing range was limited to 700 metres or less, as this was the point at which engine overheating while under water became a problem.

# OBIEKT 614A MEDIUM TANK

The Obiekt 614A project was a simple modification carried out on a number of Soviet tanks in the early 1960s to provide additional long-range anti-tank capability. Three of the new 9M14 'Malyutka' (little one) PTUR (anti-tank missiles) were mounted at the turret rear of several tank types for trials purposes. The work, which was instructed in accordance with a Council of Ministers resolution dated 18 January 1962, was carried out on the T-54A tank at Plant No. 174 under the direction of A. A. Morozov.

After testing on all then-current Soviet tanks (the T-10M, T-54A, T-55, Article 167 and T-62), the project was cancelled in 1964, as the missiles in their open mountings with only thin sheet steel protection were considered vulnerable to enemy fire, while they could not be operated when the tanks concerned were on the move.

**BOTTOM LEFT** A T-54B (or upgraded T-54A), using the training snorkel for river crossing training. This device permitted the crew to escape easily if the engine stalled underwater.

**BELOW** The mechanism used to seal the turret race and lock the turret in place for underwater crossing.

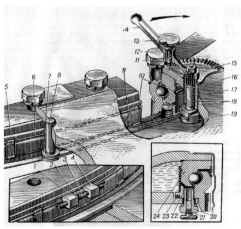

# CHAPTER FIVE
## SOVIET ARMY SERVICE AND EXPORT

The T-54 enjoyed a relatively long career in the Soviet Army and even into the early days of the reformed Russian Army, but under Soviet control the tank type only directly participated in three incidents. The first was the suppression of the Hungarian Revolution in 1956, followed by support for the construction of the Berlin Wall in August 1961, and finally Operation *Dunay* launched against Czechoslovakia in August 1968.

In the first incident most of the tanks used were T-34-85, IS-3 and T-44 types. One image has now surfaced of a T-54A burned out by Molotov cocktails by the Hungarian resistance, but there is no solid evidence of how many of these tanks participated in the operation.

In between these incidents, T-54 tanks were a major player in the biggest Soviet military exercise ever held – the 1967 'Dnepr' opposed forces exercise involving over 160,000 combat troops and other forces, primarily from the Carpathian and Belorussian Military Districts. T-54s are easy to recognize in the film coverage of that exercise, as they were the only tanks equipped with a DShKM anti-aircraft machine gun at the time. The other tanks, namely T-55s and T-62s, did not feature a similar weapon until 1972.

During the initial work on erection of the Berlin Wall, there was a tense standoff on 13 August 1961 at Checkpoint Charlie between M48 tanks of Company F, 40th Armor, Berlin Brigade, and a company of Soviet T-54s on the other side of the barrier. After a few days of staring each other down, both sides pulled their tanks back.

During Operation *Dunay* the Soviet Union sent in a number of divisions from the Group of Soviet Forces Germany and the western military districts of the Soviet Union to bring the Dubček

(Text continues on page 167)

The Soviet Union provided the Afghan Army with a number of T-54 tanks, such as the upgraded Model 1949.

**TOP LEFT** Due to both combat and units changing sides – one problem with an army where family counted more than allegiance to a nation – many T-54s used in Afghanistan constantly changed hands and fought on both sides. This T-54 Model 1949 is now in Mujahedin hands.

**TOP RIGHT** A T-54 Model 1949 in the hands of the Mujahedin. This is the same tank as above, but from this view it is seen to be fitted with additional side skirt protection.

**ABOVE** The Soviet Army initially used the T-54 in Afghanistan, but it was replaced by the T-62 later in the war. Here is a field maintenance base servicing T-54 Model 1951 tanks.

**TOP** An early T-54 crosses a small stream during a Soviet Army exercise.

**RIGHT CENTRE** Some Soviet exercises concentrated on driver training, and this T-54 Model 1949 appears to be doing just that.

**ABOVE** As noted, the Soviet Army driver training was ongoing and considered critical. Here a driver-mechanic conducts obstacle negotiation in a T-54 Model 1947.

**RIGHT BOTTOM** Soviet tankers were taught to use defilade for ambush. This remarkably well emplaced upgraded T-54 Model 1951 is being inspected by senior officers evaluating the crew efforts.

A T-54B tank from an unknown unit of 20th Guards Army of Group of Soviet Forces (GSVG) in Germany during Operation *Dunay*, Prague, August 1968. (Andrey Aksenov)

**OPPOSITE BOTTOM** The same tank as that on page 151 right centre exits the obstacle. As the tank is an upgraded T-54 Model 1947, it is mostly likely within a dedicated training unit.
**BELOW LEFT** Two T-54 Model 1947 tanks on a field exercise, probably in a training unit as the older model tanks have later running gear modifications.
**BELOW RIGHT** A T-54 Model 1947 tank driver-mechanic poses for the camera. The technical ban on such photographs was of course ignored in the Soviet Army as in all others. A typical Soviet village is in the background.

**OPPOSITE TOP LEFT** Another T-54 Model 1947 driver-mechanic takes a break. The pose is remarkably 'avant garde' though 'tanker fashion wear' never really caught on…

**OPPOSITE TOP RIGHT** Two T-54B tanks manoeuvring around tank traps during a Soviet Army exercise.

**OPPOSITE BELOW** A T-54A crew stopped for a portrait. Whether for an official photographer or the family album is unclear.

**ABOVE LEFT** A typical Soviet combined arms exercise with at least company level participation and the infantry just visible behind the tanks in the distance.

**ABOVE RIGHT** A group of tankers watch a T-54 Model 1951 negotiate a course with the driver-mechanic 'buttoned up' in the hull. Hot weather tank training was conducted in the southern republics of the Soviet Union.

**BELOW** A platoon of Soviet Army T-54A tanks undergoes road march training.

A T-54 model 1949 tank after modernization in the 1960s,
from an unknown unit of the Syrian Army in Ramtha, Jordan, during the
1970 Palestinian uprising against King Hussein (so called 'Black September').
(Andrey Aksenov)

The T-54B tank from the 202nd Tank Brigade of the
North Vietnamese Army that broke through the gates of the
Reunification Palace in Saigon on 30 April 1975. (Andrey Aksenov)

**ABOVE** A platoon of upgraded T-54 Model 1951 tanks deploying. The tank on the left has the fittings for the BTU-54 bulldozer blade.
**BELOW** A T-54A company commander receives orders from an Mi-2 helicopter during an exercise. This seemingly overly complex arrangement was frequently done both to avoid radio transmissions and to hand off map overlays to the commander.

**TOP LEFT** A platoon of upgraded T-54 Model 1951 tanks preparing for an exercise.

**TOP RIGHT** A T-54A crew standing by their tank. Soviet tank crews were in part selected according to their (lack of) height, due to relatively cramped working conditions.

**ABOVE LEFT** This appears to be a battalion of upgraded T-54 Model 1951 tanks preparing for combat on the Chinese border in 1969.

**ABOVE RIGHT** The Soviets were deeply concerned with (and trained for) chemical warfare and practised decontamination with a number of methods. Here a T-54 Model 1951 drives through a spray arch for chemical decontamination.

**BELOW** The T-54 was used during Soviet military parades. Here a battalion of upgraded T-54As or T-54Bs moves towards Red Square in Moscow, 7 November 1962. The AAMG mount has been removed for this event.

**TOP** For longer river crossings not under fire, pontoons such as the PMP would be assembled and used to float the tanks across a river. This T-54A is riding across a river in style.

**ABOVE LEFT** This T-54B is being shipped by rail and has been attached to the platform of the flat car by track locks, which are not visible in this photo.

**ABOVE CENTRE RIGHT** The T-54 was widely exported. The Syrian Army was a major user of T-54 tanks of all types, and here a T-54 Model 1949 is moving along a street.

**ABOVE RIGHT** The Vietnamese Army received a number of T-54s and used them during their war with the US. Here is a Model 1951 upgrade post-war being transported on a flatbed trailer.

**TOP LEFT** Maintenance is a necessary evil for tankers, and here the engine deck is being removed from a T-54B for work on the engine. The radiator is attached to the grille section and the two-section snorkel from the OPVT is in its final design storage location under the auxiliary fuel tanks.

**TOP RIGHT** Maintenance and training on the 12.7mm DShKM machine gun, with the sight about to be inspected.

**ABOVE** A training unit with T-54 Model 1947 tanks laying out the ammunition complement before stowage in the tanks.

**OPPOSITE TOP LEFT** Four Soviet Army officers pose with their tanks. These are T-54 Model 1949 tanks with some upgrade features such as the mixed road wheels on tank No. 602. The tanks are probably being rotated out of storage (parked under wrap on wooden beams) for exercise, as was standard in the Soviet Army.

**OPPOSITE TOP RIGHT** Tank maintenance takes place no matter what the weather conditions. This mechanic has the radiator up and is working on the transmission.

**OPPOSITE BOTTOM** The two crewmen in the engine compartment of this tank have just removed the air cleaner on the left.

**TOP LEFT** This T-54 Model 1947 has had the left rear final drive removed, probably for replacement. These tanks have been upgraded with 200-litre auxiliary fuel tank racks and 'starfish' roadwheels.

**ABOVE LEFT** A tank crew taking a break from summer maintenance, probably with their company commander (a captain). Sitting on tank barrels is learned from childhood in Russia.

**ABOVE RIGHT** If there was an operational problem with the D-10T gun in the field, a crane would be sent out to lift the turret from the rear so the gun could slide out the back of the tank for replacement or repair. This crane appears to be just starting that procedure.

**NEXT PAGES** As the Soviet Union was developing the mighty An-22 transport aircraft, with a cargo capacity of 80,000kg and a range of over 3,000km, it was tested for fit with different loads, including the T-54.

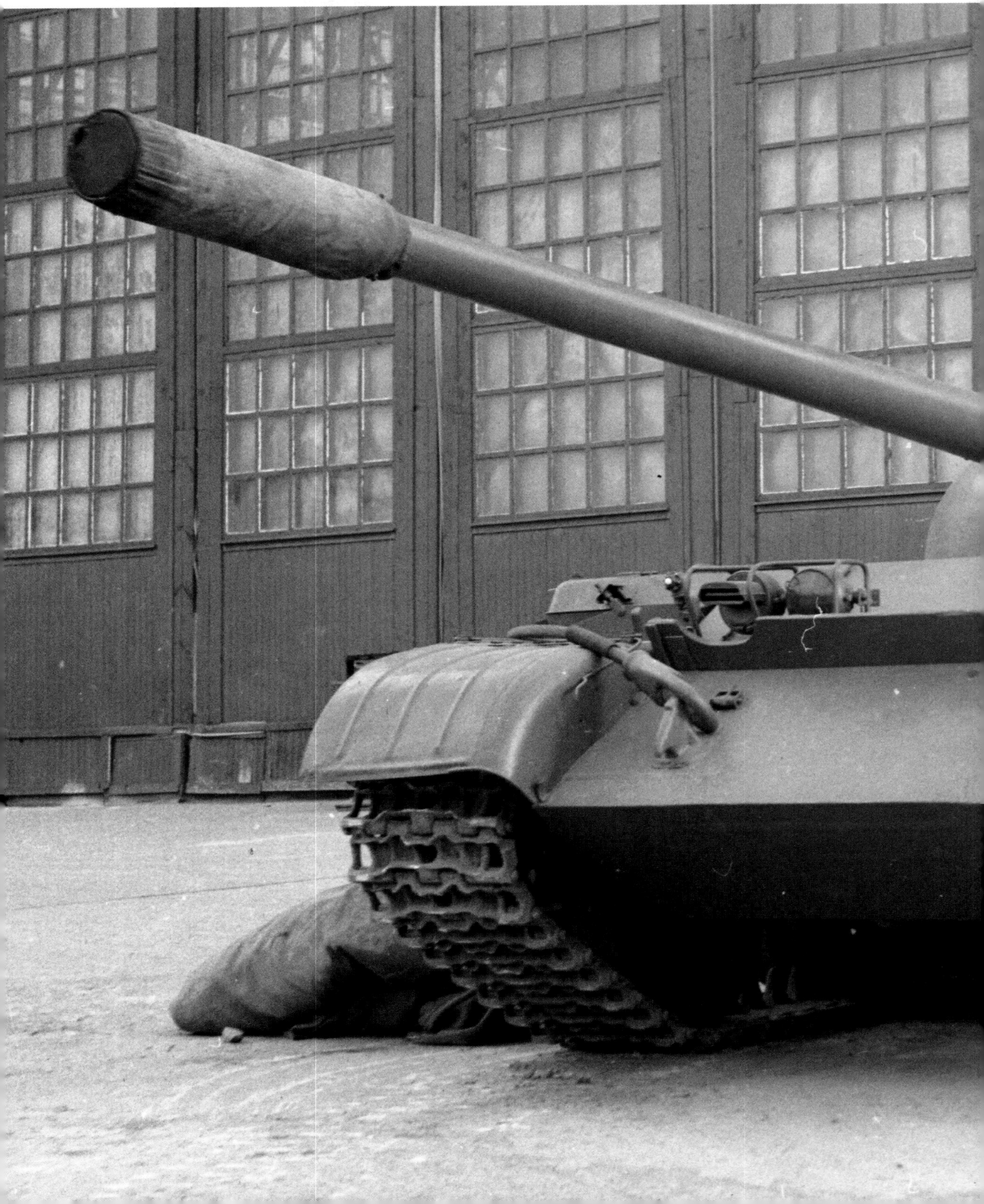

**ABOVE LEFT** This T-54A was selected for An-22 fuselage test fit trials.

**ABOVE RIGHT** The T-54A tank had all 'standard' encumbrances, such as the AAMG and rear fuel tank drums, removed before testing.

government into line with Soviet thinking. For their part the Czechs – having seen the ruins of Budapest 12 years earlier – did not want the same result for Prague and did not resist. The worst incident was when the 6th Guards Tank Division and the 7th Guards Tank Division (GTD) – both equipped with a mixture of T-54 and T-55 tanks – ran into each other. The 6th GTD had no invasion stripes and the 7th GTD did, and in the confusion the latter confused the former as being resisting Czech forces, and an engagement ensued, with several tanks destroyed before level heads intervened and stopped the engagement. The 7th GTD was sent back to Germany in disgrace and the 6th GTD presumably painted the required invasion stripes on their tanks.

One curious side note that is rarely mentioned is that when Operation *Dunay* was taking place, a Hollywood movie company was shooting the film *Bridge at Remagen* in Czechoslovakia, having been refused permission to film in Germany. The film was made near the village of Most, with the bridge scenes being filmed on the old bridge at Davle on the river Vltava that was used to simulate the famous Rhine bridge. The Hollywood movie featured a large number of American vehicles used as film props. As the 'wartime' American vehicle column was being filmed racing towards the old Vlatva bridge, the convoy ran head-on into a column of very much contemporary Soviet Army T-54 and T-55 tanks coming in the other direction. The Soviets had last heard that NATO forces, specifically the US 7th Army, were advancing in response to the Soviet intervention. As the columns met, the Soviet Army prepared to engage; however, within a few minutes it was clear to the Soviet commanders that the 'opposing' vehicles were World War II vintage vehicles with film cameras deployed on and around them, and after a short 'discussion' the Soviet armoured column passed the Hollywood actors by.

While Soviet Army T-54 tanks were constantly upgraded in service, by the 1970s they were considered second line, and most, even if updated, went into long-term strategic storage. Some Soviet tanks were reportedly upgraded with new radio equipment and engines to T-54M, T-54AM and T-54BM status, but they still remained in storage depots or were sold abroad. The service life of the T-54 tank series was formally ended in 1997, when President Yeltsin signed an order directing that all of the remaining T-54 tanks then in Russian strategic storage be scrapped.

---

**OPPOSITE ABOVE LEFT** The tank located in the An-22 cargo bay with a man provided for scale. He appears happy with this duty!

**OPPOSITE ABOVE RIGHT** The same T-54A now moved further back into the cargo hold.

**OPPOSITE CENTRE** The T-54A being driven off the An-22. The same aircraft was loaded with other tanks for trials, from the PT-76 to the T-10 heavy tank series.

**OPPOSITE BOTTOM LEFT** Another view of the T-54A in the middle of the cargo bay with a measuring stick for determining size and fit.

**OPPOSITE BOTTOM RIGHT** Another view of the tank near the rear of the cargo bay. The An-22 could transport two T-54s from a weight viewpoint, but actual fit was determined manually during these trials.

OPPOSITE TOP LEFT The T-54 is very well represented in museums and public displays in both the former Soviet Union and abroad. This relatively complete T-54A or B with RMSh tracks guards the entrance to the medium tank hall at the Kubinka Tank Museum near Moscow.

OPPOSITE TOP RIGHT This relatively pristine T-54 Model 1949 located in Ekaterinburg is another typical survivor.

OPPOSITE CENTRE LEFT Another complete T-54B is part of this display in Kiev, Ukraine. Note the gun muzzle counterweight added to early tanks fitted with later gun stabilization.

OPPOSITE CENTRE RIGHT An overhead view of the same T-54B taken from the hill behind in the above photograph.

OPPOSITE BELOW LEFT This T-54 Model 1949 is part of the Military Museum collection in Ekaterinburg.

OPPOSITE BELOW RIGHT The Vietnamese have preserved the T-54 that is reputed to have been the first one to crash through the Presidential Palace gates in Saigon (now Ho Chi Minh City), bringing the Vietnam War to a close.

OPPOSITE BOTTOM The particularly eclectic Technical Museum in Togliatti includes both a T-54 Model 1949 and an early T-72, along with many unusual vehicles.

BELOW The fabled (and now cleared) Kubinka reserve field included many prototypes not on display, including this T-54A or B with no distinguishing external features.

The T-54 was, however, a popular tank for sales to the Warsaw Pact and favoured Soviet client states, and as a result they were widely sold or sent abroad to numerous other countries. As those countries broke up or suffered from civil wars, the T-54 could frequently be found in service on both sides of some conflicts. (See the appendix for a list of customers and known users of the T-54 tank.)

In later years, Soviet-built T-54 tanks were joined in service in various countries by the Polish- and Czech-produced models, as well as the Chinese Type 59.

Probably the most iconic shot of a non-Soviet-built T-54 was when infantry on the back of T-54 tank No. 843 (followed by No. 846) of the People's Army of Viet Nam (PAVN) smashed down the gates of the Presidential Palace of the Republic of Vietnam in Saigon and summarily ended the Vietnam War. This, more than perhaps any other image of a T-54, summed up the role of the tank in the Cold War.

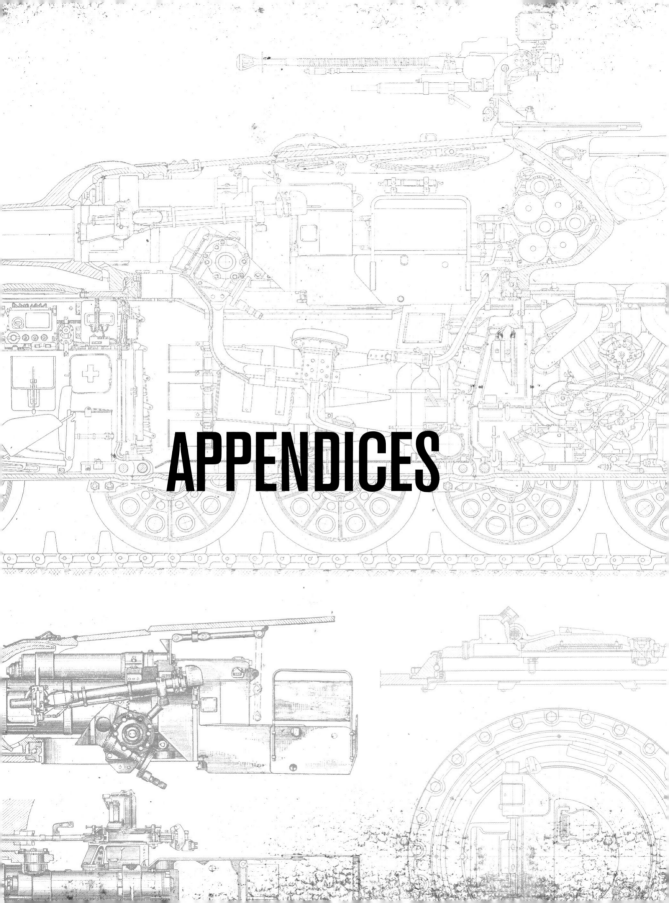

# APPENDICES

# APPENDIX ONE
## T-54 TANK PRODUCTION BY YEAR

| Year | Plant No. 183 | Plant No. 75 | Plant No. 174 | Total |
|---|---|---|---|---|
| 1945 | 1 | - | - | 1 |
| 1946 | 5 | - | - | 5 |
| 1947 | 22 | - | - | 22 |
| 1948 | 285 | 218 | 90 | 593 |
| 1949 | 29+96 | 75 | 15 | 119+96¹ |
| 1950 | 423 | 184 | 400 | 1,007 |
| 1951 | 816 | 220 | 500+30 | 1,536+30² |
| 1952 | 1,011 | 253 | 550+40 | 1,814+40² |
| 1953 | 1,135 | 280 | 540+45 | 1,955+45² |
| 1954 | 1,317 | 284 | 540+50 | 2,141+50² |
| 1955 | 1,829 | 111 | 625+50 | 2,565+50² |
| 1956 | 1,775 | 320 | 655+50 | 2,750+50² |
| 1957 | 1,007+100² | ? | ? | 1,857+100² |
| 1958 | 705+80² | ? | ? | 1,735+80² |
| Totals | 10,360+180 | 1,945+? | 3,915+?+265 | 16,220+445 |
| Grand Total (Plus 110 TO-54 and 73 fitted with PST amphibious equipment) | | | | 16,665 |
| Note: numbers do not match due to differing sources | | | | |
| 1 – Training tanks; 2 – Command (K suffix) tanks | | | | |

# APPENDIX TWO
## PRODUCTION BY TANK MODEL

| Year | Plant No. 75 | Plant No. 183 | Plant No. 174 |
|---|---|---|---|
| 1945 | | T-54 Model 1945 | |
| 1946 | | T-54 Model 1946 | |
| 1947 | | T-54 Model 1947 | |
| 1948 | T-54 Model 1947 | T-54 Model 1947 | T-54 Model 1947 |
| 1949 | T-54 Model 1947 | T-54 Model 1947, 1949 | T-54 Model 1947 |
| 1950 | T-54 Model 1949 | T-54 Model 1949 | T-54 Model 1949 |
| 1951 | T-54 Model 1951 | T-54 Model 1951 | T-54 Model 1951 |
| 1952 | T-54 Model 1951 | T-54 Model 1951 | T-54 Model 1951 |
| 1953 | T-54 Model 1951 | T-54 Model 1951 | T-54 Model 1951 |
| 1954 | T-54 Model 1951 | T-54 Model 1951, T-54A | T-54 Model 1951 |
| 1955 | T-54 Model 1951, T-54A | T-54A | T-54 Model 1951, T-54A |
| 1956 | T-54A | T-54A | T-54A |
| 1957 | T-54A | T-54A, T-54B | T-54A |
| 1958 | T-54B | T-54B, switch to T-55 | T-54B |

# APPENDIX THREE
## RELATED ARTICLE (OBIEKT) NUMBER FOR T-54 TANK DESIGNS

| Article Number | Plant Number | Vehicle and Description |
|---|---|---|
| 9 | 174 | BTS-2 high-speed tank recovery tractor |
| 55 | 174, 342 | PST-54 amphibious equipment for the T-54 tank |
| 60 | 174, 342 | PST-U amphibious equipment for the ZSU-57-2 SPAAG |
| 137 | 183, 75, 174 | T-54 tank Model 1951 (used for other early models as well) |
| 137K | 174 | T-54K Model 1951 command tank variant |
| 137G | 183, 75, 174 | T-54A tank |
| 137GK | 183 | T-54AK command tank variant |
| 137G2 | 183, 75, 174 | T-54B tank |
| 137G2K | 183 | T-54BK command tank variant |
| 137G2M | 183 | Improved T-54B tank – accepted for service as the T-55 Model 1958 (later re-designated as Obiekt 155) |
| 139 | 183, 393, 173 | T-54 tank with two-axis stabilized sight and D-54TS gun |
| 140 | 183, 393 | T-54 follow-on tank with new suspension, engine, modified hull and new turret fitted with D-54TS gun and KPVT anti-aircraft gun |
| 141 | 183, 9, 173 | T-54 fitted with D-54 high-power 100mm gun |
| 142 | 183, 9 | T-54B fitted with D-54 high-power 100mm gun |
| 413 | 75, VIU | T-54 fitted with extended front and rear mine trawl sections |
| 441 | 75 | T-54A tank with extra fittings for PAZ weapons of mass destruction protection |
| 442 | 75 | T-54A tank with TDA built-in smoke generating system |
| 481 | 75, 112 | T-54 fitted with ATO-49 flamethrower |
| 482 | 75, NII-6 | TO-54 flamethrower tank |
| 483 | 75, NII-6 | TO-54 flamethrower tank with no main gun and 1,700 litres of flame mixture |
| 486 | 75 | T-54/T-54A tanks fitted with OPVT underwater crossing equipment |
| 500 | 174 | ZSU-57-2 with twin 57mm S-68A guns |
| 510 | 174 | ZSU-57-2 fitted with amphibious flotation equipment |
| 520 | 174 | ZSU-57-2 'Dnepr' with 'Desna' electro-optic sight and 'Berezina' gun mount |
| 600 | 174 | SU-122-54 self-propelled assault gun |
| 610 | 174 | SU-122-54 with 122mm M-62T gun |
| 614A | 174 | T-54B fitted with three 9M14 'Malyutka' ATGM |
| 620 | 174 | SU-122-54 used for testing night combat equipment |

# APPENDIX FOUR
## T-54 STANDARD PRODUCTION MODEL TECHNICAL CHARACTERISTICS

| Technical Characteristic | T-54 Model 1947 | T-54 Model 1949 | T-54 Model 1951 | T-54A | T-54B |
|---|---|---|---|---|---|
| **General Data** | | | | | |
| Year Produced | 1947 | 1949 | 1951 | 1955 | 1957 |
| Combat weight metric tonnes | 34.9 | 36 | 35.5–36 | 36 | 36.4 |
| Crewmen | 4 | 4 | 4 | 4 | 4 |
| Overall Dimensions in mm Length (hull) Width Height | 8,950 (6,370) ? ? | 8,950 (6,370) 3,200 2,380 | 9,000 (6,370) 3,270 2,400 | 9,000 (6,370) 3,270 2,400 | 9,000 (6,370) 3,270 2,400 |
| Power to weight ratio (per hp/kWt) | 13.3 (9.8) | 14.4 (10.6) | 14.4 (10.6) | 14.4 (10.6) | 14.4 (10.6) |
| Ground clearance in mm | 425 (or 440) | 425 (or 440) | 425 (or 440) | 425 (or 440) | 425 (or 440) |
| **Armament** | | | | | |
| Type of gun/number | D-10T (1) | D-10T (1) | D-10T (1) | D-10TG (1) | D-10-T2S |
| Calibre in mm | 100 | 100 | 100 | 100 | 100 |
| Length of barrel in mm (calibres) | 5,600 L/56 | | | | |
| Aiming limits (degrees) Traverse Elevation | 360 +18 to -5 | 360 +18 to -5 | 360 +18 to -5 | 360 +18 to -5 | 360 +18 to -5 |
| Muzzle velocity in m/s / Weight of projectile in kg AP APDS | 895/15.88 None | 895/15.88 None | 895/15.88 None | 895/15.88 None | 895/15.88 None |
| Co-axial machine gun Number Calibre in mm Type | 1 7.62 SG-43 | 1 7.62 SG-43 | 1 7.62 SGMT | 1 7.62 SGMT | 1 7.62 PKT |
| Bow machine gun Number Calibre in mm Type | 2 (wing) 7.62 SG-43 | 1 (bow) 7.62 SG-43 | 1 (bow) 7.62 SGMT | 1 (bow) 7.62 SGMT | 1 (bow) 7.62 PKT |
| Anti-aircraft machine gun Number Calibre in mm Type | 1 12.7 DShK | 1 12.7 DShK | 1 12.7 DShK/ DShKM | 1 12.7 DShKM | 1 12.7 DShKM |
| Basic Load Main gun 7.62mm 12.7mm | 34 3,500 150 | 34 3,000 200 | 34 3,500 500 | 34 3,500 500 | 34 3,500 500 |
| Armament stabilizer | None | None | None | Gorizont – single axis | Tsiklon – two axis |
| Rangefinder – type | Reticule mask insert for both main and co-axial machine gun | | | | |

| Technical Characteristic | T-54 Model 1947 | T-54 Model 1949 | T-54 Model 1951 | T-54A | T-54B |
|---|---|---|---|---|---|
| **Armour Protection (thickness/angle of inclination from the vertical in degrees)** | | | | | |
| Hull mm/degrees | | | | | |
| Glacis | | | | | |
| Upper | 120/60 | 100/60 | 100/60 | 100/60 | 100/60 |
| Lower | 120/55 | 100/55 | 100/55 | 100/55 | 100/55 |
| Sides | 80/0 | 80/0 | 80/0 | 80/0 | 80/0 |
| Screen | None | None | None | None | None |
| Rear: | | | | | |
| Upper | 45/60 | 45/60 | 45/60 | 45/60 | 45/60 |
| Centre | 45/17 | 45/17 | 45/17 | 45/17 | 45/17 |
| Lower | 30/70 | 30/70 | 30/70 | 30/70 | 30/70 |
| Roof | 30/90; 20/90 | 30/90; 20/90 | 30/90; 20/90 | 30/90; 20/90 | 30/90; 20/90 |
| Belly | 20/90 | 20/90 | 20/90 | 20/90 | 20/90 |
| Turret mm/degrees | | | | | |
| Mantlet | n/a | n/a | n/a | n/a | n/a |
| Glacis | 200/0 | 200–108/0–60 | 200–108/0–60 | 200–108/0–60 | 200–108/0–60 |
| Sides | 160–125/0–45 | 160–86/0–60 | 160–86/0–60 | 160–86/0–60 | 160–86/0–60 |
| | | | 136–100/0–45 | 136–100/0–45 | 136–100/0–45 |
| Rear | n/a | n/a | 65–48/0–45 | 65–48/0–45 | 65–48/0–45 |
| Top | 30/81 | n/a | n/a | n/a | n/a |
| **Armour Thickness as a Shell Path** | | | | | |
| Hull mm/degrees | | | | | |
| Glacis | | | | | |
| Upper | 240 | 200 | 200 | 200 | 200 |
| Lower | 211 | 175 | 175 | 175 | 175 |
| Sides | 80 | 80 | 80 | 80 | 80 |
| Screens | None | None | None | None | None |
| Rear | | | | | |
| Upper | 90 | 90 | 90 | 90 | 90 |
| Middle | 45 | 45 | 45 | 45 | 45 |
| Lower | 88 | 88 | 88 | 88 | 88 |
| Roof | 30; 20 | 30; 20 | 30; 20 | 30; 20 | 30; 20 |
| Belly | 20 | 20 | 20 | 20 | 20 |
| Turret, mm/degrees | | | | | |
| Mantlet | n/a | n/a | n/a | n/a | n/a |
| Glacis | 200 | 200–216 | 200–216 | 200–216 | 200–216 |
| Sides | 160–179 | 160–172 | 160–172; | 160–172; | 160–172; |
| | | | 136–143 | 136–143 | 136–143 |
| Rear | n/a | n/a | 65–60 | 65–60 | 65–60 |
| Top | 30 | n/a | n/a | n/a | n/a |
| **Mobility** | | | | | |
| Top speed in km/h | 48 | 50 | 50 | 50 | 50 |
| Obstacle Negotiation | | | | | |
| Grade in degrees | 30 | 30 | 30 | 30 | 30 |
| Slope in degrees | 30 | 30 | 30 | 30 | 30 |
| Wall in metres | 0.73 | 0.73 | 0.73 | 0.73 | 0.73 |
| Ford in metres | 1.4 | 1.4 | 1.4 | 1.4 | 1.4 |
| Trench in metres | 2.7 | 2.7 | 2.7 | 2.7 | 2.7 |
| Average ground pressure in kg/cm$^2$ | 0.93 | 0.82 | 0.82 | 0.82 | 0.81 |
| Highway range in kilometres | 360–400 (with aux tanks) | 360–400 (with aux tanks) | 360–400 (with aux tanks | 440 (with tanks) | 650 (with tanks) |
| Fuel capacity in litres | 530+180 | 530+180 | 530+190 (200–400 aux) | 530+285 (200–400 aux) | 812+200/400 aux |

| Technical Characteristic | T-54 Model 1947 | T-54 Model 1949 | T-54 Model 1951 | T-54A | T-54B |
|---|---|---|---|---|---|
| **Engine-Transmission Installation** | | | | | |
| Engine – type | V-2-54 | V-54 | V-54-5 | V-54-6 | V-54B |
| Type | Diesel liquid cooled | | | | |
| Cycles | 4 | | | | |
| Number of cylinders | 12 | | | | |
| Layout | 60° V type | | | | |
| Cylinder bore in mm | 150 | | | | |
| Piston stroke in mm | 180; 186.7 | | | | |
| Maximum power hp/kWt | 520 (382) | | | | |
| RPM at maximum power | 2,000 | | | | |
| Displacement in litres | 38.88 | | | | |
| Transmission type | Mechanical | | | | |
| Torque converter | No | | | | |
| Gearbox type | Simple, mechanical | | | | |
| Number of speeds fwd /rev | 5/1 | | | | |
| Steering gear | Ribbon Brakes | Ribbon Brakes | Planetary | Planetary | Planetary |
| **Running Gear** | | | | | |
| Suspension type | Individual torsion bar | | | | |
| Shock Absorbers | None | 4 | 4 | 4 | 4 |
| Track drive | Drive sprockets located at rear of hull | | | | |
| Length of run on ground in mm | 3,840 | 3,840 | 3,840 | 3,840 | 3,840 |
| Track width in mm | 500 | 500 | 580 | 580 | 580 |
| Track pitch in mm | 137 | 137 | 137 | 137 | 137 |
| Number of links | 91 | 90 | 90 | 90 | 90 |
| Type of track hinging | Open metallic | | | | |
| Number of road wheels per side | 5 | 5 | 5 | 5 | 5 |
| Road wheels in mm (D – diameter, W – width) | 810 D 150 W | 810 D 150 W | 810 D 150 W | 810 D 165 W | 810 D 165 W |

# APPENDIX FIVE
## SOVIET STANDARDIZED PRODUCTION FLOW FOR ARMOURED VEHICLES

**1** All new projects must start with a request from the Council of Ministers and the Central Committee. These are given to the relevant factories who then decide if they can meet the project requirements. If they can, they are tasked with carrying out scientific research work on a project to determine its viability.

**2** **Scientific Design Work.** (*Nauchno-Issledivatal'naya Rabota* or NIR). This is the scientific work that can determine the feasibility of a project and lay out possible solutions to the tasking. At this stage the project either has a project name (e.g. 'Liven', 'Oka', 'Akatsiya', etc.) or a factory internal designator. Once the NIR work is approved by the Scientific Committee for the Council of Ministers the factory is then authorized to carry out prototype design work.

**3** **Prototype Design Work.** (*Opytno-Konstruktorskaya Rabota* or OKR). At this stage, the project now has an article designator or Obiekt number (e.g. Obiekt 137, Obiekt 482). This stage requires at least one running prototype of the vehicle for assessment. Depending upon the problem at hand, as many as six prototypes may be built, including one for destructive firing testing of its armour protection.

**4** **Factory Testing.** Once the prototype is ready it undergoes factory testing by the designers and engineers in concert with the customer representative – the Ministry of Defence representative to the factory. Once the major bugs have been ironed out and approval is granted by the Scientific Committee, the vehicle is then sent for State Range Testing at Kubinka.

**5** **State Range Testing.** The military and members of the Ministry of Defence and Ministry of Defence Production test all major qualities of the new vehicle in a series of planned tests at the Kubinka Test Range. 'Findings' are made, which require the factory to repair or correct them as soon as possible. Once all corrections are made, permission is granted for troop testing.

**6** **Troop Testing.** This usually requires an establishment lot (*ustavlennaya partiya*) of vehicles to be built – usually either 3, 5, 10, or 25, depending on the viability of the product and requirements for thorough testing. Vehicles may be sent to various parts of the USSR for testing – the north for winter conditions, Kazakhstan for desert conditions, the Urals for mountainous conditions, etc. Once the vehicle passes its troop testing phase, the Ministry of Defence and Ministry of Defence Production will recommend it for acceptance and full production.

**7** **State Resolution.** A joint resolution of the Central Committee of the Politburo of the Communist Party and the Council of Ministers of the USSR (many members holding positions in both) names the item (i.e. T-10, T-10A, T-10M, etc.) and announces it is accepted for service with the Red Army. Full production may then be ordered by the Ministry of Defence and Ministry of Defence Production (occasionally the project is tabled at this point due to extenuating circumstances) followed by the factory preparing to put the vehicle into full production. This may take place nearly immediately if only a modification of a vehicle in series production, or as much as a year and a half delay while the factory remodels and retools to produce the new machine. All this may take up to ten years of elapsed time from project to first production model rollout.

# APPENDIX SIX
## T-54 MODEL 1949 CUTAWAY DIAGRAM

(Andrey Aksenov)

| | | | |
|---|---|---|---|
| **1** | GST-49 night-positioning light | **27** | Unditching log |
| **2** | Front fuel tank hatch | **28** | Spare engine oil tank |
| **3** | Spare part and instrument box | **29** | Sprocket wheel |
| **4** | Turret traversing hand drive | **30** | Engine exhaust pipe |
| **5** | Turret lifting hook | **31** | V-2-54 diesel engine hatch |
| **6** | Turret traversing electric motor control | **32** | AA MG travelling locks |
| **7** | TSh-20 optical gunner's sight | **33** | D-10T cleaning tool box |
| **8** | D-10T 100mm gun | **34** | Turret bustle ammunition rack |
| **9** | Gun mantlet | **35** | Tank commander's seat |
| **10** | TPKU commander's visor | **36** | D-10T gun breech |
| **11** | Commander cupola hatch | **37** | 10-RT-26 radio |
| **12** | Turret ventilator dome | **38** | Gunner's seat |
| **13** | 12.7mm spare ammunition box | **39** | Driver's hatch |
| **14** | DShKM MG ammunition box | **40** | 'Spider-web' type wheel |
| **15** | DShKM 12.7mm MG | **41** | Track link |
| **16** | DShKM MG anti-aircraft sight housing | **42** | Idler wheel |
| **17** | External fuel tanks | **43** | Spare track links |
| **18** | Turret ammunition stowage | **44** | Driver's seat |
| **19** | Engine air filter hatch | **45** | Driver's clutch control |
| **20** | Turret handle | **46** | Gearbox lever |
| **21** | Loader's hatch with AA MG turret | **47** | Hull SGMT 7.62mm MG aperture |
| **22** | Radiator armoured cover | **48** | Saw |
| **23** | Engine fan cover | **49** | Wooden splash guard |
| **24** | Engine fan armoured flap | **50** | Towing hook |
| **25** | MDSh smoke canisters | **51** | Headlight |
| **26** | Towing cable | | |

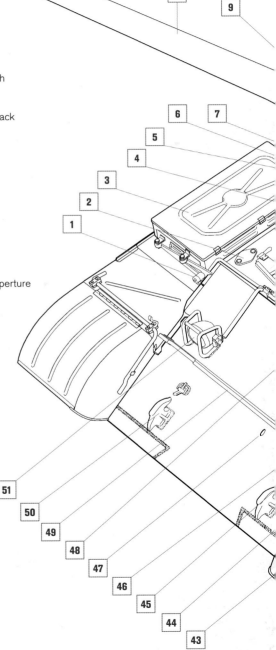

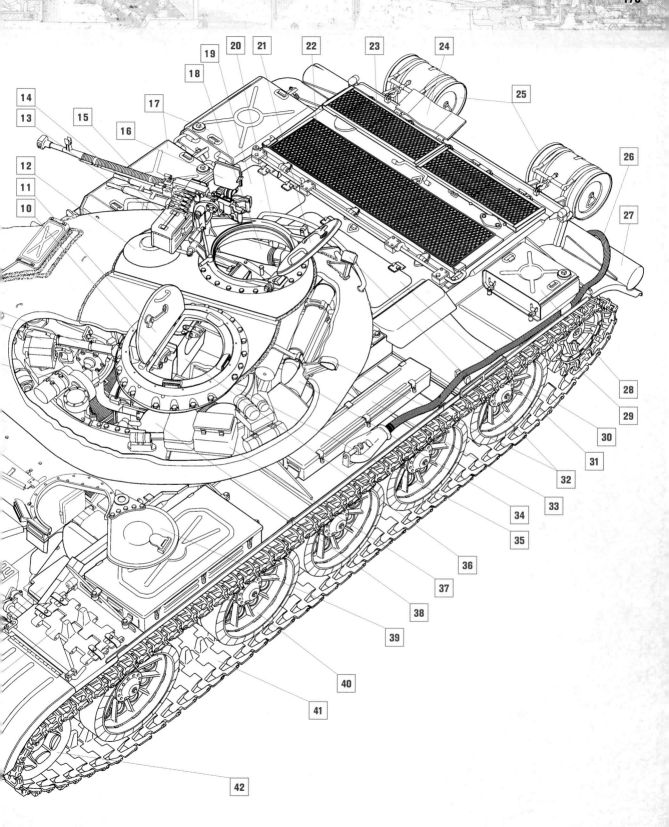

# APPENDIX SEVEN
## GLOSSARY

| | |
|---|---|
| **APU:** | Auxiliary Power Unit |
| **BO:** | Boyevaya Otdel – fighting compartment |
| **BTS:** | Bronyevoy Tyagach Srednyy or Srednyy Tankovyy Tyagach – Medium Tank Tractor |
| **ChKZ:** | Chelyabinsky Kirovskiy Zavod (ChTZ from 15.05.58) |
| **ChTZ:** | Chelyabinsky Traktorniy Zavod imeni V.I. Lenina (ChKZ before 15.05.58) |
| **GBTU:** | Main Armoured Vehicle Directorate |
| **GABTU:** | Main Automotive and Armoured Vehicle Directorate |
| **LKZ:** | Leningrad 'Kirov' Factory (also Factory No 185) |
| **LVZ:** | Leningrad 'Voroshilov' Factory (later Factory No 174 in Omsk) |
| **KB:** | Konstruktorskoye Buro – design bureau |
| **KO:** | Kontrol'naya Otdel – control compartment |
| **MBT:** | Main Battle Tank |
| **MO:** | Ministerstvo Oboroni – Soviet (Russian) Ministry of Defence (MoD) |
| **MOP:** | Ministerstvo Oboronoi Promishlennosti – Soviet (Russian) MoD Production |
| **MTO:** | Motorno-Transmissionaya Otdel – motor transmission compartment |
| **MTrM:** | Ministerstvo Trasportnogo Mashinostroenya (Ministry of Transport Machinery Construction) |
| **NTK:** | Nauchno-Tekhnicheskiy Komitet (Scientific Technical Committee) |
| **OKMO:** | Opytniy Konstruktorsko-Mekhanicheskiy Otdel – Prototype Design Mechanical Section |
| **OPVT:** | Oborudovaniye Podvodnoy Vozhdeniya Tanki – underwater tank driving equipment |
| **PAZ:** | Protivoatomnoi Zashiti – anti-nuclear protection |
| **PPO:** | Protivo-Pozharnoye Oborudovaniye – fire suppression equipment |
| **PTURS:** | Protivo-Tankovye Upravlyaaemye Raketnye Systemy – ATGM system |
| **PU:** | Puskovaya Ustanovka (launch system) |
| **SM SSSR:** | Soviet Ministerov SSSR – Council of Ministers of the USSR |
| **TsK KPSU:** | Central Committee of the Communist Party of the Soviet Union |

A T-54 model 1951 tank of the Reserve Officers School in Hamina, Finland.
All vehicles in the Finnish Army got three-tone 'splinter' camouflage in 1981. (Andrey Aksenov)

| TPU: | Tankovoe Peregovornoe Ustroistva – tank verbal communications system |
|---|---|
| UVZ: | Uralsky Vagonostroitelny Zavod (Urals Railway Wagon Construction Factory) |
| VPK: | Voenniy Promishlennoi Kommissiei pri Soviet Ministrov SSSR – Military-Industrial Commissariat for the Council of Ministers of the USSR |
| Zavod No. 9: | Artillery Factory No 9, Perm (F. F. Petrov Bureau) |
| Zavod No. 75: | Kharkov Tank Factory (formerly Kharkov Diesel Engine Construction Factory) |
| Zavod No. 174: | Omsk Tank Factory (formerly in Leningrad) |
| Zavod No. 183: | Urals Railway Wagon Construction Factory, Nizhny Tagil (formerly Kharkov Steam Locomotive Construction Factory in Kharkov) |
| Zavod No. 393: | Krasnogorsk Mechanical Plant (KMZ), Moscow |
| TsNII-6: | Central Scientific Research Institutes for Flame Weapons, Moscow |
| TsNII-173: | Central Scientific Research Institute for Artillery Stabilizers, Moscow |
| VNII-100: | Vsesoyuzny Nauchno-Issledovatelsky Institut (later VNII Transmash) |

# APPENDIX EIGHT
## KNOWN CUSTOMERS AND USERS OF THE T-54 MEDIUM TANK

| Country | Number | Remarks |
| --- | --- | --- |
| Afghanistan | 250 | Ordered from the USSR from ex-Soviet Army stocks. Delivered in a batch of 50 and a batch of 200 |
| Albania | 75 | T-54s from the USSR – now out of service |
| Algeria | 165 | Ordered from the USSR in batches of 40, 25 and 100 |
| Angola | 150+ | Mixed lot of T-54 and T-55 tanks, later supplemented by ex-Czech and Polish tanks |
| Bangladesh | 15 | Ex-Egyptian tanks |
| Bosnia and Herzegovina | 13+ | Accumulated by various sources over the years |
| Bulgaria | 850 | Ordered from the USSR in 1953 – now out of service |
| Cambodia | 10 | Ordered from the USSR in 1983 |
| Chile | 4 | Captured Syrian tanks ordered from Israel for familiarization |
| CSSR | 2,700* | Some purchased from the USSR but most domestically produced |
| Republic of the Congo | 25(-) | Mixed origin collection of T-54 and T-55 tanks |
| DPRK | 700 | T-54 tanks ordered from the USSR in two batches |
| East Germany | 202 | Ordered from the USSR; 488 additional T-54A and T-54AM tanks of Polish manufacture purchased at a later date with T-54A tanks upgraded to T-54AM level. 648 T-54AM tanks remained in service at the end of the German Democratic Republic |
| Egypt | 350 | Ordered in 1961 – most likely of Czech manufacture |
| Ethiopia | 260(-) | Mixed order of ex-service T-54 and T-55 tanks from the USSR |
| Finland | 50 | Ordered from the USSR in 1960 |
| Georgia | 120(-) | Mixed order of T-54s and T-55AM2 tanks from the Czech Republic |
| Guinea | 8 | Ordered in 1974 from the USSR |
| India | 300 | Ordered from the USSR in 1954; later supplemented by 274 Czech-built T-54 tanks |
| Iran | 60 | T-54s purchased from Libya in 1981 |
| Iraq | 300+ | Ordered in 1958 and 1967 from the USSR as well as some from other users |
| Israel | 1,500(-) | Captured tanks from the 1967 and 1973 wars – rebuilt first as Ti-67 tanks and then as Tiran 4 tanks (mixed T-54 and T-55 tank types) |
| Kurdistan | ? | About 250 ex-Iraqi Army T-54, T-55 and Type 69 tanks in service |
| Laos | 15 | Ordered from the USSR in 1973 |
| Lebanon | 180(-) | Ordered from Syria in 1991 – ex-Soviet tanks |
| Libya | 800 | Ordered from the USSR in three batches – 1970, 1975 and 1976 |
| Mali | 12 | T-54s still in service |
| Mongolia | 250 | Ordered from the USSR in 1960 |
| Morocco | 40 | Ordered from the USSR in 1960 (T-54B) and later supplemented by 80 T-54 tanks from Czech production |
| Mozambique | 60 | Ordered from the USSR in 1981 |
| Nicaragua | 20 | Ordered from the USSR in 1984 |
| Pakistan | 100 | Ordered from the USSR in 1968 |
| Peru | 24 | Ordered from the USSR in 1973 |
| Poland | 3,000* | Some from the USSR but most tanks of domestic production – some later upgraded to T-54AM standards |
| Rwanda | 24 | Mixed stocks of T-54 and T-55 tanks |
| Somalia | 135 | 100 ordered from the USSR in 1972 and 35 purchased from Egypt in 1977 |
| SRV | 400 | Ordered from the USSR in 1969 |
| Sudan | 50 | Ordered from the USSR in 1969 |
| Syria | 850 | Ordered from the USSR in 1958, 1967 and 1978 |
| Tanzania | 32 | Ordered from East Germany in 1979 |
| Togo | 2 | Ordered from Egypt |
| Uganda | 16 | Ordered from the USSR in 1974 |
| Yugoslavia | 160 | Ordered from the USSR – migrated to subsequent independent countries |
| Zambia | 5 | Ordered from the USSR in 1975 |
| Zimbabwe | 20 | Ordered from the USSR in 1984 |

*Note The CSSR and Poland were licensed producers of the T 54 and made a number of modifications to their models that differentiated them from Soviet tanks. Plus signs mean more than that number is likely, minus signs that they are part of a mixed reporting of T 54 and T 55 tanks. Many of the tanks were lost or destroyed in various conflicts and most of the numbers presented here indicate only their initial known holdings.

# APPENDIX NINE
## OPVT UNDERWATER TANK DRIVING EQUIPMENT

Since tanks obviously do not float as designed, tank designers in the 1930s and 1940s worked on methods to permit them to cross water obstacles of relatively narrow span and shallow depth. The Germans developed a system for their Pz.Kpfw. III tanks in the planned invasion of Great Britain called 'Tauschpanzer' (Diving Tank), which sealed the tank and provided an air intake via a floating flexible snorkel. While they used it to cross some rivers with moderate success, it was never a standardized feature.

In the post-war era, designers at UVZ – after doing terrain analysis of Western Europe where a water obstacle is encountered roughly every 15–20km but most are less than 5 metres deep – began work on a method to permit their tanks to cross such obstacles without either swimming equipment (bulky and awkward) or assault bridging (difficult under fire). The results of these developments were fielded with the final production versions of the T-54B tank, and then immediately adapted for use on the T-55.

The equipment – *Oborudovaniye dlya Podvodnogo Vozhdenniya Tanka* (OPVT) or 'Equipment for Underwater Driving of Tanks' – began to be issued in early 1958. Its purpose was to permit the so-fitted tank to autonomously cross a water obstacle of up to 700 metres' width with a depth of 5 metres or less and also permit the tank to emerge from the water in a combat ready status. The system provided air to the crew and engine, prevented water from flooding and stalling the engine while underwater, ensured the tank could move underwater in a given direction, and ensured the tank was completely mobile when it came out of the water.

To this end the OPVT system consisted of a number of components:

- A two-section snorkel tube roughly 3.5 metres long when assembled;
- An exhaust flapper valve providing one-way exhaust flow;
- Covers for the radiator air intake;
- Covers for the gun muzzle, gunner's sight aperture, machine gun port, and antenna feed and base;
- Cover for the air feed to the transfer case ('guitara');
- Sealing for the turret, ventilator, ZIP bins and hatches;
- Life jackets and re-breathers for crew escape if necessary;
- A GPK-48 gyrocompass for underwater navigation.

The idea was to carry all of this equipment on the tank, but it was not obvious that was entirely possible. The major problem item was the two-section snorkel, which even in collapsed state was about 1.75 metres long and 15cm in diameter. It was eventually installed in brackets on top of the 200-litre auxiliary fuel tanks on production tanks and under them in later conversions of T-54 Model 1949, Model 1951 and T-54A tanks.

To prepare the tank for crossing, all of the seals were checked first and drain plugs installed in the hull floor of the tank. The snorkel was removed and bolted together with seals between sections and base, the loader's MK-4 viewer was removed from its mount, and the assembled snorkel was attached with bolts in its place. Steps were bolted to the snorkel for the use of rescue personnel to climb up and contact the crew via yelling down the tube if the tank stalled. The covers were attached to their specific items with clamps and the flapper valve installed to the exhaust outlet.

The entire engine deck area was covered by a rubber-impregnated canvas cover, which was bolted down to the edges of a frame. There was a fixed metal frame in the middle with a folding and sealing hatch cover to permit airflow on land without removing the cover. The engine radiator air intake had five moveable internal louvres that could be adjusted to cut off outside airflow while the cover prevented water ingress.

Once the tank was prepared, a seal around the inside of the turret race was inflated to prevent water entry into the tank. Some leakage was expected during the crossing and charts told the crew what was acceptable; once the tank had completed the crossing a bilge pump could be turned on to evacuate water that did seep into the tank.

The actual crossing usually required prepared banks on both sides of the obstacle, or at least shallow approaches to the river or stream. The tank would move into the water at 1500rpm in first gear to make the crossing. The driver-mechanic would thereafter use the GPK-48 gyrocompass to keep the tank heading in the right direction. Once across, the tank could fire on targets immediately if needed, but this would destroy the muzzle and machine gun covers. The tank would start to overheat if the hatch over the engine deck was not opened soon after crossing, and the tanks could not sit at idle for a long time with no air circulation.

For night crossings a cable would be dropped down the snorkel and a red light similar to the standard tank marker and tail-lights fitted to the top so the commander could follow the progress of his tanks across the water.

There were accidents during training and exercises, and quite often tow cables would be attached to tanks to ensure that if they stalled they could be hauled out. Often (as in East Germany) the places where training took place were concrete structures to make it easy to enter, cross and exit.

Several changes took place over the years. One was the introduction of a larger training snorkel that bolted to the commander's cupola and allowed the crew easy egress if the tank stalled underwater. Another was an antenna feed to the top of the snorkel so training commanders could speak to the tank via radio. Both were for the safety of the crew and also to reduce the number of accidents. If the driver-mechanic did not switch on the GPK-48 to give him a bearing, the worst potential problem was that the tank would turn 90° toward downstream and go with the flow rather than across it.

# BIBLIOGRAPHY

## BOOKS – RUSSIAN LANGUAGE

Baryatinskiy, Mikhail, *1945–2008: Sovetskiye Tanki v Boyu* (Yauza/Ehksmo, 2008)

Baryatinskiy, Mikhail, *Sredniy Tank T-34: Vsya Pravda o Proslavlennom Tanke* (Yauza/Ehksmo, 2009)

Baryatinskiy, Mikhail, *Tanki XX Vek – Unikal'naya Ehtsiklopediya* (Yauza/Ehksmo, 2010)

Baryatinskiy, Mikhail, Kolomiyets, Maksim, and Baushev, I. (editor), *Sozdateli Oruzhiya I Voyennoy Tekhniki Sukhoputnykh Voysk Rossii* (Pashkov Dom, Moscow, 2008)

Bryukhov, Vasiliy P., *Bronetankovye Voyska* (Golos Press, Moscow, 2006)

Chernyshev, Vladimir L. (editor), *Tanki I Lyudi: Dnevnik Glavnogo Konstruktora Aleksandra Aleksandrovicha Morozova*, http://www.btvt.narod.ru, 2006/2007 (translated by author)

Daynes, Vladimir, *Bronetankovye Voyska Krasnoy Armii*, (Yauza/Ehksmo, 2009)

Drogovoz, Igor G., *Tankovyy Mech SSSR 1945–1991* (P'yedestal, 1999)

Drogovoz, Igor G., *Tankovyy Mech Strany Sovetov* (Kharvest, Minsk, 2001)

Fes'kov, V. I., Kalashnikov, K. A. and Golikov, V. I., *Sovetskaya Armiya v Gody 'Kholodnoy Voyny' (1945–1991)* (Tomsk State University, Tomsk, 2004)

Ionin, S. N., *Bronetankovye Voyska SSSR-Rossii* (Veche, Moscow, 2006)

Karpenko, A. V., *Obozreniye Otechestvennoy Bronetankovoy Tekhniki (1905–1995 gg.)* (Nevskiy Bastion, St Petersburg, 1996)

Kholyavskiy, G. L., *Ehtsiklopediya Bronyetekhniki – Gusenichnye Boyevye Mashiny* (Kharvest, Minsk, 2001)

Kolomiyets, Maksim, *Nasledniki 'Tridtsat' Chetverki' T-34M, T-43, T-34-100, T-44* (Yauza/Ehksmo, 2012)

Kolomiyets, Maksim and Moshchanskiy, Il'ya, *Armada Vertikal' No. 5: Kamuflyazh Tankov Krasnoy Armii 1930–1945* (Exprint, 1999) (translated by the author in 1999 for the 2000 printing in English)

Lavrenov, S. Ya., *Sovetskiy Soyuz v Lokal'nykh Voynakh I Konfliktakh* (Astrel', Moscow, 2003)

Minayev, A. V. (general editor), *Sovetskaya Voyennaya Moshch: Ot Stalina do Gorbacheva* (Voyennyy Parad, 1999)

Ministry of Defence Publications, *Rukovodstvo po Ehksplotatsii Tanka T-44* (Moscow, 1946)

Ministry of Defence Publications, *Rukovodstvo po Material'noy Chasti I Ehkspluatsii Tanka T-55* (Moscow, 1969)

Moskovskiy, A. G. (general editor), *75 Let Upravleniyu Nachal'nika Vooruzheniya* (Voyennyy Parad, Moscow, 2004)

Pavlov, M., Pavlov, I. and Zheltov, I., *Neizvestnyy T-34* (Exprint, Moscow, 2001)

Polonskiy, V. A. (chairman of the editorial group), *Glavnoye Avtobronyetankovoye Upraveniye: Lyudi, Sobytiya, Fakty v Dokumentakh 1943–1944 gg.*, Book III (Ministry of Defence of the Russian Federation, Moscow, 2006)

Polonskiy, V. A. (chairman of the editorial group), *Glavnoye Avtobronyetankovoye Upraveniye: Lyudi, Sobytiya, Fakty v Dokumentakh 1944–1945 gg.*, Book IV (Ministry of Defence of the Russian Federation, Moscow, 2007)

Polonskiy, V. A. (chairman of the editorial group), *Glavnoye Avtobronyetankovoye Upraveniye: Lyudi, Sobytiya, Fakty v Dokumentakh 1946–1953 gg.*, Book V (Ministry of Defence of the Russian Federation, Moscow, 2007)

Rogoza, S. L. and Achkasov, N. B., *Zasekrechennye Voyny 1950-2000 gg* (AST, St Petersburg, 2004)

Safonov, B. S. and Murakhovskiy, V. I., *Osnovnye Boyevye Tanki* (Arsenal-Press, Moscow, 1993)

Solyankin, A. G., Pavlov, M. V., Pavlov, I. V. and Zheltov, I. G., *Otechestvennye Bronirovannye Mashiny XX Vek: Tom 2 - Otechestvennye Bronirovannye Mashiny 1941–1945* (Exprint, Moscow, 2005)

Solyankin, A. G., Zheltov, I. G. and Kudryashov, K. N., *Otechestvennye Bronirovannye Mashiny XX Vek: Tom 3 - Otechestvennye Bronirovannye Mashiny 1945–1965* (Tseykhgauz, Moscow, 2010)

Svirin, Mikhail, *Armada Vertikal' No. 4: Artilleriyskoye Vooruzheniye Sovetskikh Tankov 1940–1945* (Exprint, 1999)

Svirin, Mikhail, *Tankovaya Moshch' SSSR : Pervaya Polnaya Ehntsiklopediya* (Yauza/Ehksmo, 2009)

Ustyantsev, Sergey and Kolmakov, Dmitriy, *Boyevye Mashiny Uralvagonzavoda: Tank T-34* (Dom 'Media-Print', Nizhny Tagil, 2005), Part 1 (translated by author)

Ustyantsev, Sergey and Kolmakov, Dmitriy, *Boyevye Mashiny Uralvagonzavoda: Tanki T-54/T55* (Dom 'Media-Print', Nizhny Tagil, 2006), Part 3 (translated by author)

Ustyantsev, Sergey and Kolmakov, Dmitriy, *Boyevye Mashiny Uralvagonzavoda: Tanki 60-ikh* (Dom 'Media-Print', Nizhny Tagil, 2007), Part 4 (translated by author)

Vasilyeva, Larisa and Zheltov, Igor, *Nikolay Kucherenko: Pyat'desyat Let v Bitve za Tanki SSSR* (Atlantida – XXI Vek/Moskovskiye Uchebniki, 2009) (translated by author)

Vasilyeva, Larisa, Zheltov, Igor and; Chikova, Galina, *Pravda o Tanka T-34* (Atlantida – XXI Vek/Moskovskiye Uchebniki, 2005) (translated by author)

Veretrennikov, Aleksandr, Rasskazov, Igor, Sidorov, Konstantin and Reshetilo, Yevgeniy, *Kharkovskoye Konstruktorskoye Byuro po Mashinostroyeniyu imeni A. A. Morozova* (IRIS Press, Kharkov, 1998)

Veretrennikov, Aleksandr, Rasskazov, Igor, Sidorov, Konstantin and Reshetilo, Yevgeniy, *Kharkovskoye Konstruktorskoye Byuro po Mashinostroyeniyu imeni A. A. Morozova* (Kharkov, 2007)

## BOOKS – ENGLISH LANGUAGE

Magnewski, Janusz, *Combat Vehicles of the People's Polish Armed Forces 1943–1983* (FBIS Translation, October 1989)

Hull, Andrew, Markov, David and Zaloga, Steven, *Soviet/Russian Armor and Artillery Design Practices: 1945 to the Present* (Darlington Publications, Darlington, Maryland, MD, 1999)

Scott, Harriet F. and Scott, William F., *The Armed Forces of the USSR* (Westview Press, Boulder, CO, 1979)

## PERIODICALS – RUSSIAN LANGUAGE

*Bronekollektiysa* (Moscow)
    *No. 3/1999 – Srednyy Tank T-34* – Mikhail Baryatinskiy
    *No. 4/1999 – Srednyy Tank T-34-85* – Mikhail Baryatinskiy
    *No. 3/2003 – T-34 – Istoriya Tanka* – Mikhail Baryatinskiy
*Krasnaya Zvezda* (Moscow)
*Modelist-Konstruktor* (Moscow)
*M-Khobbi* (Moscow)
*Tekhnika i Oruzhiye* (Moscow)
*Tekhnika i Vooruzheniye* (pre-1991 Soviet issues)
*Tekhnika i Vooruzheniye: Vchera, Segondya, Zavtra* (Moscow)
    Continuing Series by M. V. Pavlov and I. V Pavlov:
    *Otechestvennye Bronirovannye Mashiny 1945–1965 gg.*


## PERIODICALS – GERMAN LANGUAGE

*Miltaer & Geschichte*, August 2017, pp. 38–45, "Der Exportschalger" –
    Clemens Niesner


## PERIODICALS – ENGLISH LANGUAGE

*Armor* (US Army)
*AFV Profile* (London)
    *No. 23 – Soviet Mediums T44, T54, T55 & T62* – Major Michael Norman
*International Defence Review*
*Jane's Defence Review*


## ONLINE SOURCES

'Gur Khan Attacks' – http://gurkhan.blogspot.com/
'Soldat.ru' – http://www.soldat.ru/
'Yuri Pasholok's Journal' – http://yuripasholok.livejournal.com/

# INDEX